·······the COMPLETE·······
EXCUSES
·······HANDBOOK·······

by LOU HARRY and JULIA SPALDING

CIDER MILL
PRESS

BOOK
PUBLISHERS

KENNEBUNKPORT, MAINE

13 Digit ISBN: 978-1-933662-80-0
10 Digit ISBN: 1-933662-80-8

This book may be ordered by mail from the publisher. Please include $2.00 for postage and handling.Please support your local bookseller first!

Books published by Cider Mill Press Book Publishers are available at special discounts for bulk purchases in the United States by corporations, institutions, and other organizations. For more information, please contact the publisher.

Cider Mill Press Book Publishers
"Where good books are ready for press"
12 Port Farm Road
Kennebunkport, Maine 04046

Visit us on the web!
www.cidermillpress.com

Design by Jessica Disbrow

Printed in China

1 2 3 4 5 6 7 8 9 0
First Edition

➡ DEDICATION

This book is humbly dedicated to David Dinkins, former New York City mayor, who answered accusations that he failed to pay his taxes by stating: "I haven't committed a crime. What I did was fail to comply with the law." Or maybe we should dedicate it to writer Henry Miller, whose wife caught him in a compromising position with her best friend. Miller's excuse for later leaving his wife: "I couldn't tolerate being married to a woman who didn't trust me." Then there's the Tour de France's Floyd Landis who said the only reason why his steroid test turned up positive was because...

You know what? Let's just dedicate this book to every dog that has ever been accused of eating someone's homework.

→ TABLE OF CONTENTS

INTRODUCTION 6
HOW TO USE THIS BOOK 7
HOW NOT TO USE THIS BOOK 8

EXCUSES BY CATEGORY
The General EXCUSE 10
Excuses for ABSENCE/AVOIDANCE 16
Excuses for ARTISTS AND CELEBRITIES 24
Excuses for BAILING OUT ON SOMEONE 32
Excuses for BEING THE OTHER WOMAN/OTHER MAN 36
Excuses for CONSUMING JUNK 40
DATING Excuses 46
GAMBLING Excuses 52
Excuses for GENERAL STUPIDITY 58
Excuses for NOT BEING AS GENEROUS AS YOU COULD 64
Excuses for HOUSEHOLD ISSUES 68
ICONIC Excuses 74
Excuses for KIDS 82
Excuses for LATENESS 86
Excuses for LEAVING EARLY 92
Excuses for LEGAL MATTERS 96
    -Minor Infractions 98
    -Major Infractions 101
MEDICAL Excuses 108

ODIFEROUS Excuses 116

Excuses for OVEREATING/NOT EXERCISING 122

Excuses for PARENTS 130

Excuses for PARTYING HARD 134

PERSONAL RELATIONSHIP Excuses 140

POLITICAL Excuses 146

RANDOM Excuses 154

SCHOOL/EDUCATION Excuses 164

S-E-X Excuses 170

Excuses Related to SHOPPING AND RETAIL 176

SPORTS Excuses 184

TECHNOLOGICAL Excuses 192

Excuses for TELLING A SECRET................................. 196

WORKPLACE Excuses 200

Excuses UTTERED BY THE RICH AND SHAMELESS 206

APPENDIX: Miscellaneous Excuse Stuff 210

    About Excuses 210

    Monosyllabic Excuses 212

    The Musical Excuse Mix Tape 213

INDEX TO MAJOR EXCUSES 214

ABOUT THE AUTHORS... 224

➡ INTRODUCTION

This book is not our fault.

Seriously.

It really isn't.

We were minding our own business, when we received a call from a publisher—this book's publisher, to be exact.

He had an idea.

That idea: Create the definitive guide to excuses good and bad, large and small. Since we all have them—and we've all used them—why not exhaustively catalogue and celebrate them? And considering the universal appeal of an airtight explanation for why we do (or do not do) the things we do, there would certainly be a broad readership for such a tome.

We hope that you, after reading this book, decide not only that the publisher's idea was a very good one, but also that his idea of selecting us to write it was also a good one.

But even if you decide that the idea itself was not a good one—or that selecting us to execute it was not a good one—just keep in mind, as we said earlier, it's not our fault.

How to
USE THIS BOOK

There are a number of effective ways to get the most out of this book.

One way is to browse randomly for ideas that may come in handy in the future. After all, it's difficult for an excuse to be effective if it doesn't roll trippingly from the tongue at the precise moment that it is needed.

Another way is to refer to the Table of Contents, which has been arranged by type of excuse. If you need to make an excuse about a slip-up at work, you'll want to turn to WORKPLACE excuses. If you are perpetually late, you can look through Excuses for LATENESS. Or say, for example, you are approached by a man on the street and you're not sure if he's shady or down on his luck. What you do know is that you would really rather spend your last $5 on a blended mocha than a handout. In that case, you would flip to Excuses for NOT BEING AS GENEROUS AS YOU COULD and browse those options.

A third way to use this book is to go straight to the index, where the excuses are listed alphabetically. Find a line that sounds good, learn a little more about it, and give it a try. Easy peasy!

How NOT TO USE THIS BOOK

As evidence in a court of law. As a flotation device. As a doorstop. As kindling. As a tool to teach English to the foreign-born. As a bribe. As barter for pelts. As a way to find a mate. As an indictment of our public education system.

The
GENERAL
EXCUSE

While many excuses apply to only narrow sets of circumstances, others cover a much broader field. Some of them are pretty darn near close to universal, usable in just about any situation.

There tend to be two possible outcomes from the use of the general excuse.

One is that the matter at hand is dismissed without further ado. We refer to this as The Desirable Option.

The other is known as The Undesirable Option. This happens when the excused-to party realizes that you didn't even care enough about the matter to take the time to fashion an excuse that involved specifics. It is usually followed by drastically lowered expectations of your ability to handle just about anything.

While there will always be a temptation to use one of these rather than craft something more creative, apply them judiciously.

➡ I AM WHAT I AM

You have to admire an excuse that is so flexible it has been used by everyone from God to Popeye to the drag queen in the musical La Cage aux Folles. This tautological bit of simplicity is both concise and difficult to argue with. Of course, God, Popeye and that particular drag queen never had to answer for themselves in court.

➡ I DIDN'T GET A CHANCE

Confessing that time wasn't on your side begs the question of what else you did besides the task at hand. This holds much more power if it is accompanied by the knowledge of all the other hard work or do-goodness that you did with your time (i.e., I didn't get a chance … I was too busy saving little old ladies from the burning convalescent home) rather than the more likely circumstance (i.e., There was a Diff'rent Strokes marathon on Nick at Nite).

➡ I DIDN'T GET ENOUGH LOVE AS A CHILD

Pity the child starved for childhood affection. But while you're at it, pity the employer, spouse, neighbor or anyone else who has to deal with the wearing-it-as-an-excuse-for-everything sad sack.

➡ I FORGOT

It does happen. In fact, it happens more than we would like to admit. It is, believe it or not, one of the most popular excuses when people are caught trying to bring firearms onto airplanes (Come to think of it, what else are you going to say?) and one of the lamest—but most accurate—defenses for missing a loved one's birthday or, often even worse, your own wedding anniversary.

➡ I HAD A BAD DAY

It would be perfectly acceptable and reasonable—in almost all cases—to respond to this statement with "So what?" Yet most of the time, the Bad Day plea is the excuse equivalent of a Get Out of Jail Free card. Keep in mind, however, that people will label you a flake if you try to throw your own personal pitty party every single day that something is expected of you.

➡ I WAS DRUNK

This catch-all for just about any bad behavior—from minor indiscretions to inexcusable offenses—is evoked more often than just about any other excuse. It's pulled out when Mel Gibson offers up an anti-Semitic rant or when your roommate realizes that the previous night's liaison was with a partner resembling the Creature from the Black Lagoon.

While this excuse usually places one somewhere in the range of criminal to pathetic, there is an upside to it if you use it as an excuse for trying something positive that you otherwise might not have tried—flirting with someone above your station, for instance. Or belting out a karaoke tune.

Then again, you might want to scratch that last one. Did you ever hear a drunken karaoke rat destroy "Unchained Melody?"

➡ I'LL TRY ANYTHING ONCE

There are, in actuality, only a handful of people who do anything only once. These are usually people who either do grievous harm to themselves or get arrested after doing that thing a single time.

Most of us do things more than once. We try them and we keep at it. Even if we don't particularly like it—few smokers, for instance, have a great experience the first time out. We still adhere to the "try, try again" idea after the lack of success on the first shot.

And so when we say "I'll try anything once," we usually mean, "I have no really good reason for doing this, but someone brought up the idea, and my desire isn't necessarily to do it or to not do it—but to not not do it. So I'll do it."

And so you do it.

Probably not a good move.

Still, this pre-emptive strike gives you some credit for at least warning those around you that the results have, at least for you, no precedent.

➡ I'M NOT FEELING WELL

A nice, non-specific universal excuse, good for getting out of heavy lifting or staying home from a particularly difficult class. It also has a proven track record of helping put an early end to bad blind dates.

➡ I'M WORKING ON IT

While using this excuse, you lead others to believe that there's still hope for you. Of course, you'll need a different excuse when you fail to deliver later.

➡ IT'S NOT MY FAULT

Ah, the pesky little thing known as fault. It often seems as if the human species is hardwired to not take responsibility for its actions. Even if caught red-handed, our minds race toward explanations that don't involve our own culpability. Fault, this line implies, lies not with the doer, but with all of those people and circumstances that have influenced the doer. Not me. I'm clean.

The subtext of this, though, is that the accused, while possibly still at some fault, has found someone whose fault is greater, deflection being a key element in good excuse-making.

The effectiveness of this excuse is largely contingent on the amount of evidence available of your involvement in the incident. Best to hold it for situations in which there are no third-party witnesses or forensic proof.

➡ LIFE'S TOO SHORT

Okay, there are plenty of books and websites out there about the things you should do before you shuffle off this mortal coil. And if this excuse helps you to break out of your routine and do something truly memorable, interesting, self-defining, worthwhile and/or out of the ordinary, then more power to you.

The problem comes when you use this excuse as a way of rationalizing doing something that is likely to shorten your life even further.

SOME ADDITIONAL
GENERAL EXCUSES
TO ADD TO YOUR REPERTOIRE

➤ IF I DON'T DO THIS, MY BIOGRAPHER WON'T HAVE MUCH TO WRITE ABOUT.

➤ IT'LL MAKE A GREAT STORY TO TELL JAY LENO.

➤ WHEN YOU'RE AN INTERNATIONAL SPY, YOU CAN'T QUESTION YOUR ASSIGNMENT. YOU JUST DO IT AND LET THE CHIPS FALL WHERE THEY MAY.

➤ YOU WOULDN'T ACCUSE ME OF THAT IF YOU KNEW OF MY LINEAGE.

EXCUSES FOR ABSENCE/ AVOIDANCE

You're supposed to be there.

You're not there.

That's a problem.

When you don't show up where or when you're expected, you need an arsenal of excuses at the ready to take the focus off your glaring omission.

➡ I FELL ASLEEP

Everyone sleeps. Therefore, everyone understands the lure of some shuteye. But not everyone has a lot of sympathy for your claim to have zonked out when you were expected elsewhere, especially when everyone else who managed to show up as promised wouldn't have minded getting a few extra winks themselves.

➡ I FORGOT IT WAS DAYLIGHT SAVINGS TIME

This excuse can come in handy once—maybe twice—a year.

➡ I GOT THE DATE WRONG

There are, at last count, seven days in a week. Any given month has between 28 and 31 days. It really isn't that difficult to find the square on your calendar or the button on your blackberry that corresponds to the day you are making plans for.

Still, getting the day wrong gives you more of an excuse to completely miss something. One hyper-apologetic phone call and a little self-deprecation should be enough to get you through until you botch another appointment.

➡ I HAD A DOCTOR'S APPOINTMENT

This old standby has the added bonus of giving you the option of following it up with a well-documented illness excuse. The value of the excuse shifts depending on your station in life. In elementary and high school, it's usually invalid without some sort of note. At the college level, however, it's usually invalid with or without a note because the professor doesn't give a damn—and one half-hour doc visit shouldn't keep you from completing an assignment. And why didn't you schedule it for a time when you didn't have class, huh? It might be a bit more effective when trying to get out of a sports practice, but then you run the risk of being "that guy."

In the working world, the doc appointment excuse works fairly easily. The problem comes if you don't actually have an appointment this time … but the following week, when you actually are sick, you've got some creative explaining to do—which isn't easy with a 102-degree fever.

In the social world, the doc appointment excuse is near foolproof—except that it isn't valid on Saturdays, Sundays and evenings, which most likely rules out your entire social life.

➡ I WAS IN THE SHOWER

The problem when using this diversion from a phone call or knock on the door is that showers only last so long. Unless you're a human prune (or Howard Hughes), you really can't expect people to believe that you were under the spigot for the entire three hours that they were trying to get you on the horn.

➡ I WASN'T GETTING A SIGNAL

Until the telecommunications superpowers figure out a way to provide us hapless civilians with reliable cell phone service, we're going to be able to pull this one out as a way out of making an uncomfortable call. If you live in an area that's full of canyons, you can get a lot of mileage out of this excuse. (See also: The Signal is Breaking Up.)

➡ I'M FASTING

Trying to get out of dining with someone? Announce your observance of an obscure ethnic holiday—we like the two-week fast leading up to the Dormition of the Theotokos (from the Eastern Orthodox faith)—and end the conversation as quickly as possible.

➡ I'M HAVING A BAD HAIR DAY

Sympathy for this judgement-call excuse largely depends on one's own coif-challenged nature. Something that many people do not understand, however, is that Bad Hair Day has a deep, dark subtext that, when understood by the recipient, can give you a great deal of forgiveness. The fact that your hair is not looking its best was probably just the straw that broke the camel's back. The real tragedy (which should merit carte blanche clemency) is more of an incremental calamity. You woke up late, didn't have time to shower, found a zit on your nose and a run in your last pair of pantyhose, spent 15 minutes looking for your car keys, and then ran into your ex with his new fiancé at Starbucks.

So you went home and got back in bed.

➡ IT'S THE FIRST NICE DAY

With the coming of spring comes the coming of the temptation to blow off work or school. On that first beautiful day, who wants to be confined to a desk? Of course, if you review the employee or student manual, you won't find any reference to this being an acceptable excuse for absence, so don't even try it on anyone with authority.

➡ MY ALARM MUST HAVE BEEN BROKEN

The alarm clock has been around since about the 15th century, and small bedside alarm clocks have been popular since the 1870s. Which means that, if you had an early morning meeting during, say, the Dark Ages (600-1100-ish AD), you might have an excuse for arriving a few minutes late. After that, however, you're trying the patience of the person who has been waiting and waiting and waiting (unless, of course, there's been a power failure—in which case that would have been your excuse).

Most people know that the proper BS-to-English translation of "My alarm clock must have broken" is "I screwed up in setting the alarm" or "I forgot to set the damn thing," or, most commonly, "I hit the snooze button seven times."

➡ MY CAR DOORS WERE FROZEN SHUT

This is a good one to use in extreme weather conditions when you've already exhausted the Traffic Was at a Crawl excuse. Keep in mind that car doors freezing shut is strictly a sub-32-degree problem, so you'll need to make sure the weatherman backs you up. Better yet, this excuse is most buyable if at least one other person in your party had the same issue.

➡ MY PHONE MUST HAVE BEEN OFF THE HOOK

Note how this excuse subtly blames the technology rather than the excuse-maker. Note, too, how, with cordless phones the norm and answering machines as common as refrigerators, this is rapidly loosing its cache as a valid excuse for missing a call.

➡ THERE WAS A DEATH IN THE FAMILY

Pull out this excuse only in the most desperate of circumstances. For if such a thing as karma exists, it will surely come back to you after you fake the death of a loved one. Out-of-town relatives are, of course, preferred, since they are more difficult to track and less likely to require extensive cover stories that could be disproved.

➡ TRAFFIC WAS AT A CRAWL

Whether you modify this one with a tale of a bad accident or particularly icy roads, blaming other motorists is a tried and true out—making certain, of course, that the person you are telling it to doesn't travel the same route as you do.

SOME ADDITIONAL
ABSENCE/
AVOIDANCE
EXCUSES TO ADD TO YOUR REPERTOIRE

➤ I DIDN'T REALIZE IT WAS MORE IMPORTANT TO BE HERE THAN TO SAVE A BUSLOAD OF ORPHANS.

➤ EVERYTHING WAS ON SCHEDULE UNTIL I HIT THAT WRINKLE IN THE TIME/SPACE CONTINUUM.

➤ I GOT DOUBLES FOR THE THIRD TIME AND HAD TO GO TO JAIL.

➤ IN A DEEP, SPIRITUAL WAY, I WAS THERE.

EXCUSES FOR

ARTISTS

and

CELEBRITIES

Celebrities are a special breed of people and, as such, deserve their own set of excuses applicable to the situations that they and only they become involved in.

➡ THE CAMERA ADDS 10 POUNDS

There might be some accuracy to the favorite excuse of not-quite-happy-with-their-appearance television personalities everywhere. If, however, we're talking about a newly pudgy celebrity, then it's fairly obvious to everyone that the camera is taking the fall for too many late-night crème brulees from room service.

➡ I HAD BAD REPRESENTATION

If your agent is going to take a big percentage of your paychecks, he or she might as well take some of the blame for your own bad choices.

➡ I WAS DISTRACTED BY THE PAPARAZZI

Photographers who traffic in images of celebrities coming and going from nightclubs are a much-hated lot—even though they produce what a significant number of consumers want to see. Because of the degree of hatred generated by this profession, blaming paparazzi has become an accepted excuse for all sorts of otherwise inappropriate behavior, from offering the one-finger salute to pulling a Sean Penn.

➡ I THOUGHT IT WOULD BE GOOD FOR MY CAREER

Well, we suppose doing blow with a junior casting director could help you out at some point. But it sure isn't the most dignified way to the top.

➡ I WAS DOING RESEARCH

Got caught in an FBI sting? Stopped for a broken tail light on Hollywood Boulevard while driving a cross-dressing hooker home? Wife wondering why you're frequenting Jumbo's Clown Room or playing poker for weekends at a time?

Actors and writers can always fall back on the excuse that they are doing research for an important new project. You can't create without knowledge, right? Right?

➡ I'M NOT A SELL-OUT

A common excuse among self-defined "artists" for not being able to create anything that anyone wants to pay money for.

➡ IT'S TRUE TO THE CHARACTER/IT'S IN GOOD TASTE/IT'S ARTISTICALLY VALID

Show us a decent actor trying to rationalize doing a nude scene and we'll show you someone who has trotted out this phrase—or something close to it—during an interview.

It's not just the struggling-actor-needing-to-do-this-in-order-to-get-into-the-biz demographic. Seasoned, award-winning actors have also dropped trou and/or blou, including Sir Laurence Oliver, Helen Mirran, Julie Andrews, John Malkovich, and the young woman from The Princess Diaries. Nicole Kidman, Morgan Fairchild, the guy from the Harry Potter movies, and many more serious (or serious-ish) actors have gone starkers on stage.

No matter how serious the actor may be about the artistic intent, however, the reality is that audiences are more likely to think "So that's what Angelina Jolie's ta-tas look like" rather than appreciate the depth of characterization.

➡ IT'S WHAT PEOPLE WANT

Entertainment and media folk love to revert to this one when trying to rationalize coverage of Paris Hilton, TV shows in which people eat bugs, and movies that try to find new ways to slice and dice the human body. In a sense, they are correct: If their products didn't generate an audience and, thus, make money, nobody would bother making more of their ilk.

Plus, how else are you going to explain yourself when, back in Toledo for Thanksgiving dinner, your in-laws ask why you've used your degree from NYU to produce reality shows for E!?

➡ I'VE GOT A LOT OF IRONS IN THE FIRE

When an actor, writer, or director has a lot of time between imdb.com listings, this bit of vagary gets called into action, usually followed by "Something could pop at any minute."

➡ MY HANDLERS TOOK EVERYTHING I HAD

Pint-size celebrities from Jackie Coogan (Chaplin's The Kid) to the Brothers Culkin to the inimitable Gary Coleman have used this excuse, a very, very believable story when it's coming from a former child star with an empty bank account. People tend to buy into it, even if said former child star squandered his teen years drinking tequila and smoking his body weight in whatever substance he could find. If there's one thing that's universal in the entertainment world, it's the distrust the general public has for parents, managers and others who hang on the coat-tails of famous kids.

And mimes. It's pretty universal that nobody likes mimes. Beside the point, though.

SOME ADDITIONAL EXCUSES FOR
ARTISTS AND CELEBRITIES
TO ADD TO YOUR REPERTOIRE
(Assuming, of course, that you are an artist or celebrity)

➤ I CAN'T TELL YOU OR THE SCIENTOLOGISTS WILL KILL ME.

➤ IT'S PART OF KABALLAH.

➤ STEVEN SPIELBERG IS INVOLVED WITH IT.

➤ IT'S THE NEXT BIG THING.

➤ MY AGENT STRONGLY ENCOURAGED ME TO DO IT.

➤ I PROTEST BIG OIL COMPANIES WHILE TRAVELLING IN MY FUEL-INEFFICIENT PRIVATE PLANE AND STRETCH LIMO BECAUSE, ER, WELL, EH ... I HAVE A HEADACHE. GOT TO GO.

➤ I'M MADONNA. I CAN DO WHATEVER I WANT.

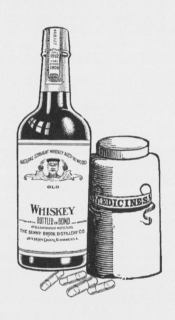

···· EXCUSES FOR ····
BAILING OUT
····· on someone ·····

You really don't want to let your buddy down. Really you don't. It's just that sometimes life gets in the way of your commitments. Hopefully, your friends will understand. Bear in mind that your excuse is easier to swallow if you catch the person you're bailing on before he leaves for the club.

➡ I DON'T HAVE ANYTHING TO WEAR

You can't expect to walk away from this classic copout with your credibility intact. Claiming that your wardrobe is keeping you from participating is not much better than saying you need to stay home to shampoo your hair or watch a movie on Lifetime.

➡ I THINK I HAVE MONO

Anyone who has ever suffered through the weeks and months of nausea, chills and debilitating malaise associated with mononucleosis will tell you that there is no "I think I have" when it comes to "mono." When you have it, you know it. And considering the symptoms can linger for up to several months, this copout calls for a long-term commitment.

➡ I THREW MY BACK OUT

Lucky for you, enough people have experienced that particular blinding jolt of pain and months of ginger recovery that you'll probably be pardoned from any obligation with a sympathetic "there-but-by-the-grace-of-God-walk-I" wince.

➡ I'M STILL HUNG OVER FROM LAST NIGHT

This excuse plays beautifully on people's insecurities. Saying that you can't go out tonight because you're still feeling the burn from your last bacchanal gives you a "been there, done that" swagger that commands respect. Rather than regarding you as the sloppy drunk that you are, they'll look to you as a worldly and socially gifted hot commodity who, incidentally, can't hold her liquor.

➡ THE SIGNAL IS BREAKING UP

The ubiquitous excuse for getting out of the middle of a cell phone call, this rising star is difficult to dispute because all of us have been stuck in those "can you hear me now?" dead zones. Of course, it doesn't go very far in explaining why you didn't call back as soon as you got to a better spot. (See also: I Wasn't Getting a Signal.)

SOME ADDITIONAL EXCUSES FOR

BAILING OUT ON SOMEONE

TO ADD TO YOUR REPERTOIRE

➤ I'VE GOT TO SEE A MAN ABOUT A DOG.

➤ MY SHOES ARE ABOUT TO EXPIRE.

➤ I'D LOVE TO, BUT I NEVER MISS A PBS PLEDGE BREAK BROADCAST.

➤ DID YOU HEAR A KETTLE? I HEARD A KETTLE. GOT TO GO.

➤ I'M ALLERGIC TO AWKWARD MOMENTS.

➤ I THOUGHT YOU MEANT 9 A.M.

···· EXCUSES FOR BEING THE ····
OTHER WOMAN/OTHER MAN

You know that icky feeling you get when you try to explain to your friends why you're breaking one of the basic rules of dating (not to mention, one of the Ten Commandments)? We call that guilt. Regardless of how solid you think your reasoning is for messing around with thy neighbor's wife/husband, prepare yourself for a hard sell.

➡ HE AND HIS GIRLFRIEND HAVEN'T BEEN GETTING ALONG

You don't have to be Dr. Phil to see right though this line, which has to rank as one of the all-time lamest excuses for—let's be honest here—being an accessory to someone's cheatin' heart. If he's so miserable with his current girlfriend, why's he still with her, huh? Your friends might nod their heads copasetically when you insist that you are the one he really wants to be with, but you lose credibility points for pulling this one.

➡ HER HUSBAND'S A WORKAHOLIC

Maybe so. But on your pool boy salary, will you be able to give her the lifestyle to which she has grown accustomed?

➡ HE'S GOING THROUGH A SEPARATION

Ah yes, that conveniently hazy state of affairs known as the separation. It's more serious than "not getting along" and yet less committal than a divorce. The man in the middle of a separation can get away with bad behavior. It's almost expected of him. Woe to the woman who gets caught in the maelstrom and has to offer up this hollow excuse when the topic comes up during Girls Night Out.

➡ SHE DOESN'T DESERVE HIM

Poor guy. Must be tough putting up with a significant other who makes him do things like answer for his behavior and make sure his undershirt lands in the hamper. Good thing he has you (his devoted woman-in-the-wings) to keep his standards comfortably below par.

SOME ADDITIONAL EXCUSES FOR *being the* OTHER WOMAN/ OTHER MAN TO ADD TO YOUR REPERTOIRE

➤ I'M TESTING OUT THIS WHOLE POLYAMORY THING I SAW ON HBO.

➤ I'M AN OLD-SCHOOL MORMON.

➤ I MAY NOT HAVE SEEN HIM FIRST, BUT I SAW HIM BEST.

➤ NANCY REAGAN WASN'T RONNIE'S FIRST.

➤ I HAVE SEEN HIS FUTURE AND SHE'S NOT IN IT.

EXCUSES FOR
CONSUMING
JUNK

Not even the most intellectual among us can live on a steady diet of highbrow entertainment. But when caught enjoying absolute garbage—be it found in books, on TV, or in your grocer's freezer—you sometimes have to cover yourself with an explanation. And that explanation is more difficult to come up with when your eyes are glazed over from a Gilligan's Island marathon.

➡ I'M RESEARCHING A PAPER FOR MY POP CULTURE CLASS

The sad thing is, at just about every college in America, you can find a class where reruns of The Facts of Life, the novels of Danielle Steele and/or the music of Yanni are legitimate topics for academic research.

➡ IT'S JUST A GUILTY PLEASURE

When you're caught watching Baywatch, listening to Barry Manilow or secretly enjoying a bowl of Spaghetti-Os for lunch, you can always resort to proudly claiming them as guilty pleasures.

➡ THERE WAS NOTHING ELSE ON

Your grandparents, who had to chose between NBC, CBS, ABC and PBS (and if you—and they—are really old, then throw in the Dumont Network), may have gotten away with this one. But you, my friend, have a remote. And, if a few trips through the 100-plus channel spectrum don't turn up anything, you've got a DVD player. And maybe even TiVo. So don't expect any sympathy when you are caught watching Real World reruns.

SOME ADDITIONAL EXCUSES FOR

CONSUMING

JUNK

TO ADD TO YOUR REPERTOIRE

➤ THE [PRODUCERS OF THIS SHOW/WRITERS OF THIS BOOK/MAKERS OF THIS SUGAR-COATED CEREAL] HID CLUES IN HERE TO A SECRET TREASURE. AND INTELLIGENTSIA BE DAMNED, I'M GOING TO FIND IT.

➤ THE PERSON WHO WROTE THIS WENT ON TO WIN THE NATIONAL BOOK AWARD.

➤ I MUST HAVE FALLEN ASLEEP DURING THE SYMPHONY CONCERT THAT WAS ON EARLIER—BEFORE THIS EPISODE OF THE GIRLS NEXT DOOR.

➤ I MAKE SOME EXTRA MONEY AS A QUALITY-CONTROL PRODUCT TESTER. BUT I'M REALLY NOT ALLOWED TO TALK ABOUT IT.

➤ THE DOCTOR SAYS I'M NOT GETTING ENOUGH SALT.

➤ BELIEVE ME, I WISH I COULD PICK THE BOOKS I'M ASSIGNED TO REVIEW.

DATING
EXCUSES

Even a good date—with a potentially right person—can go bad. The right excuse can help get you through the awkward moments and allow both of you to write off a bad experience without writing off the entire relationship. The wrong excuse, on the other hand, can insure a night that ends with, "Maybe I'll see you around sometime."

➡ I COULDN'T GET TICKETS

She wants to go to the show. You'd rather stick needles in your ears. This fake-out tries to do double duty—getting you out of the dreaded event while also showing yourself to be a wonderful person who tries so hard to make her happy. Problem is, with few concerts hitting the true sold-out status, all it really says is that her happiness isn't worth what the ticket brokers are demanding.

➡ I KNEW I SHOULD HAVE STOPPED FOR GAS

Wait. Are you serious? Did you really just try the "I ran out of gas" line? And did you really think that she was going to fall for it? And are you now trying to make some excuse for why you've shut your car off on some dark side street? Have some pride, man.

➡ IT MUST HAVE DEMAGNETIZED

When it comes time to pick up the tab and the waiter uncomfortably tells you that your credit card wasn't accepted, there's little to do except recite this ATM-generation warhorse. Just hope your guest's card isn't "demagnetized" as well. And get your account straightened out before the next date.

➡ IT SCORED BIG AT ROTTENTOMATOES.COM

Bad movies often happen to good people. But if one is putting a damper on a big date, you can simultaneously blame this popular movie website (which collects reviews from around the country and assigns a letter grade) while also showing that you did your homework in selecting this dreck

➠ I'VE GOT TWO LEFT FEET

Shy about heading out to the dance floor? This nonsensical excuse is just another way of saying "I look like an idiot out there."

➠ THEY MUST HAVE CHANGED CHEFS

First date almost ruined by surly service, lousy food, and such small portions? Pretend the restaurant has gone downhill.

➠ THIS GUITAR IS SO OUT OF TUNE

Serenading your date has an almost aphrodisiacal effect. A few sour chords can take your efforts in the exact opposite direction. When your version of Brown-eyed Girl sounds like something you'd hear on Our Gang's Greatest Hits, blame it on the instrument.

➠ YOU HAVE SOMETHING ON YOUR BLOUSE, RIGHT THERE ... OH, IT'S GONE

Okay, so you were caught staring at her breasts. There's not much you can do about it but try this, hope for the best, and for the rest of the evening keep your eyes on the ... eyes.

SOME ADDITIONAL
DATING
EXCUSES
TO ADD TO YOUR REPERTOIRE

➤ I'M SORRY. I WAS CONFUSING THIS WITH MY LAST NIGHTMARE DATE.

➤ I MUST HAVE MISTYPED. I MEANT TO SAY I'M 67 YEARS OLD, NOT 27 YEARS OLD.

➤ I ADMIRE THE ART OF DANCE IN ALL ITS FORMS. GOT ANY SINGLES?

➤ I DID TOO LET YOU USE THE MOUSE.

➤ ON THE CONTRARY, I THOUGH IT WENT VERY WELL. YOU AND I HAD A GOOD TIME AND MY MOTHER GOT A CHANCE TO GET OUT FOR SOME AIR.

➤ JUST BE THANKFUL I DIDN'T GO WITH PLAN A.

➤ I'M SORRY. THE WATCHFUL EYE OF MY PAROLE OFFICER DISTRACTED ME.

GAMBLING
·······EXCUSES·······

Winning requires no excuse. Losing, however, is a different story. The losing gambler is filled with reasons why the game didn't go in the right direction. Rarely are these excuses based on the truth, which is that gambling—at least institutionalized wagering at casinos, at racetracks, on the lottery, etc.—is designed so that you lose. It's reason for being is to make money from you.

In short, there are really, really good reasons why the Bellagio is bigger than your house.

So how do you explain your vanished bankroll, your stack of ATM withdrawal slips, your missing watch?

➡ AS LONG AS YOU'RE PLAYING, YOU GET FREE DRINKS

True enough in many a casino. But some simple math establishes that, at the rate you're going, these drinks are going to be more expensive by the ounce than Chanel No. 5.

➡ BUT I WAS WINNING

When the final out is made in the bottom of the ninth, when the time runs out in the last quarter, when the final putt lands on the 18th hole, the game is over and it is clear to all who the winner is.

For most gamblers, though, there isn't such a clear ending. There's always another game, and when your chip stack is on the rise, it's impossible to know if you are at a plateau ready for another climb or at a peak ready for a downward plummet. While there are gamblers who face bad luck from the beginning, there are a large number who, at least at one point in the playing sessions, were ahead of the game. They were winning.

But they kept playing.

As such, this excuse doesn't explain much of anything—only that you didn't know when to quit. Winners aren't winners until they walk out of the building (and, in some cases, get on a plane and go home).

➡ I HAD A RUN OF BAD LUCK

Even professional gamblers (and there aren't really that many of them outside of poker) will acknowledge that some days the cards, the dice, or the ponies don't go their way. The difference between you and a professional gambler, though, is that the pro is more likely to know how to balance his or her bankroll. A pro knows when to get out. A pro has built a financial system to absorb the swings in luck.

More importantly, the pro can always go to a more inexpensive table to find "fish" (aka suckers) to get more money to play again. Your run of bad luck may generate some sympathy—as long as your retirement fund didn't run with it.

➡ I HAVE A SYSTEM

No matter how many books claim to show you how to tap into the system, nobody has a system for beating slot machines. These machines don't have a memory, so your chance of hitting a winner this time has nothing to do with the last time the machine paid out a jackpot. Same thing with a roulette wheel. Three reds in a row doesn't mean that this time the ball is more likely to land on black. Craps? Books may help you understand how the game is played, but they won't help you beat the house edge. Even such popular system as the Martingale—which tells you to double every bet after a loss—has been statistically proven to lose you money.

All you are saying with this excuse is that you know nothing about math.

SOME ADDITIONAL
GAMBLING EXCUSES
TO ADD TO YOUR REPERTOIRE

➤ CRAPS? I THOUGHT IT WAS YAHTZEE.

➤ A SENIOR CITIZEN STOLE MY COIN CUP.

➤ I JUST GO FOR THE BUFFET.

➤ I HAVE TO SEE WAYNE NEWTON BEFORE I DIE
(OR BEFORE HE DIES, WHICHEVER)

➤ I KNEW I SHOULDN'T HAVE THROWN THAT
BLACK CAT UNDER THE LADDER AND INTO
THE MIRROR.

- **APPARENTLY, I'M ALLERGIC TO ACES.**

- **THESE TITTY TASSELS MUST BE IMPAIRING MY JUDGMENT.**

EXCUSES FOR
GENERAL STUPIDITY

There are some situations where you find yourself making less-than-stellar choices. There are other situations where the circumstances themselves reek of stupidity.

In each of them, all but the most sociopathic specimens have an understanding that they are treading in dangerous, idiotic territory. What makes the subsequent excuse more challenging is that so does everybody else.

➡ I COULD WIN A PRIZE

Radio morning show deejays are notorious for dangling a few concert tickets in front of listeners in order to get them to do all sorts of otherwise unacceptable things. And television shows from Fear Factor to The Bachelor up the ante to, respectively, big bucks and a big wedding.

➡ I WAS DARED

Who among us has not had his resolve softened by the three little words "I", "Dare" and "You"?

Yet, when the damage is done and the post-event analysis clearly indicates that you've made a horse's ass out of yourself (and possibly wound up with a scar you'll be lying about for decades), this excuse doesn't get you very far. And the older you get, the weaker it gets.

Of course, if it was a double-dog dare, then you were perfectly justified in doing whatever stupid thing you did.

➡ I WAS GOING THROUGH AN EXPERIMENTAL PHASE

This particular wording caught on at about the same time that "I was trying to find myself" lost its panache. It means basically the same thing. If you need to explain away a past indiscretion—be that a brush with the law, a few years in a commune, or feathered bangs—you can claim that you were merely dabbling in something new and exciting at the time. Now you know better. Now you have perspective. And the only regret you have is that you didn't destroy all the evidence.

➡ I WAS IN COLLEGE

True, the standard four years of higher education are infused with al-cohol-induced experimentation. Something about soaking up the last vestiges of pre-adulthood makes things like sawing the floor out of your rental so that you can have a basement with cathedral ceilings sound like a good idea. And looking back, it does sound quite charming.

➡ I WAS ON SPRING BREAK

If Las Vegas' recent motto can be "What happens in Vegas stays in Ve-gas," the slogan of spring break could be "You might want what happens on spring break to stay at spring break, but the reality is that you could be stuck with a criminal record, an uncomfortable itch, an unexplain-able tattoo, a stalker from Des Moines who you don't remember talking to (although maybe he was the guy next to you during that contest at that one bar), and/or a person who will soon be calling you 'Mom'"

Kind of difficult to fit onto a T-shirt, but you get the idea. Using spring break as an excuse for letting loose a bit is nearly universally accepted—after all, even the Amish have their rumspringa tradition of letting their bonnets down—provided that the damage to property, reputation and your future is minor.

➡ IT WAS SUPPOSED TO BE A JOKE

Obviously someone else didn't think so. This one often gets called up when a stupid comment is made that hurts another person's feel-ings. Its effectiveness depends on how quickly you can convince the other person that you really don't think he's "so fat that his favorite food is seconds."

➡ I'VE BEEN TAKING COLD MEDICINE/ I'M ON ANTIBIOTICS

For minor incidents of loopy behavior, try this excuse, get plenty of rest, and apologize again in the morning.

SOME ADDITIONAL
GENERAL EXCUSES
TO ADD TO YOUR REPERTOIRE

➤ WHAT DID YOU EXPECT FROM A CERTIFIED IDIOT?

➤ SHHHH. WE'RE BEING FILMED FOR A REALITY TV SHOW.

➤ I'M TRYING TO WIN MY FIRST DARWIN AWARD.

➤ EVERYTHING I NEEDED TO KNOW I LEARNED FROM DUMB AND DUMBER.

EXCUSES FOR
NOT BEING AS
GENEROUS
AS YOU COULD

We work hard for our money. You do, too.

So when an opportunity arises to give it away, there's a legitimate hesitation. Yet some excuses for not sharing the wealth are better than others.

➥ HE'S JUST GOING TO SPEND IT ON DRUGS OR BOOZE

It is an awkward moment. A person who may or may not be homeless extends a hand for some change. You don't want to give it. But your conscience demands that you give yourself and/or those you are with some kind of reason for your apparent inhumanity.

So you go for the drugs/booze line—which may or may not be truth. The problem isn't so much the accuracy or inaccuracy, but the almost automatic air of superiority that goes with it—the presumption that you know what someone is or isn't going to do with the cash.

➥ I DIDN'T NEED HAND-OUTS

Want to come across as It's a Wonderful Life's Mr. Potter? Try spouting this excuse when you need an excuse for not helping out those less fortunate than yourself.

➥ I GAVE AT THE OFFICE

Long since transforming from excuse to cliché, this one hasn't worked since 1964 or so. Consider: When was the last time you did any charitable donation at the office short of giving in to the boss' pressure to contribute to the United Way—or buying a couple of boxes of cookies from a Girl Scout's mom (which, of course, never make it home)?

➥ I NO SPEAK ENGLISH

Kind of pathetic, but dodging a panhandler by pretending to be a foreigner will get you a few steps further on the sidewalk—but you aren't fooling anybody. For added fun, just say, "I'm sorry. I don't speak English." Without a trace of an accent.

➡ MONEY DOESN'T GROW ON TREES

A truism, of course. And one that parents are genetically predisposed to stating whenever a hand is out for financing for anything that said parent finds frivolous.

➡ SURE, SIGN ME UP FOR (CLICK)

The next time a phone solicitor calls you when you're trying to eat dinner, go along with the spiel just long enough to hang up on yourself in the middle of your own sentence. Then, don't answer your phone for the next 15 minutes to give the phone tree long enough to give up and move on to another name. Passive aggressive? You bet. But it works.

SOME ADDITIONAL EXCUSES FOR
NOT BEING GENEROUS
TO ADD TO YOUR REPERTOIRE

➤ **HOLES IN MY POCKETS, SORRY.**

➤ **ALL MY MONEY IS TIED UP IN GOVERNMENT SECURED HIGH-YIELD BONDS.**

➤ **IF I GAVE A DOLLAR TO YOU, I'D HAVE TO GIVE IT TO EVERYBODY ON THE PLANET. AND WHERE WOULD THAT GET ME, HUH?**

➤ **THANKS EASTER BUNNY, BWOK, BWOK!**

➤ **DO YOU TAKE CANADIAN PENNIES?**

EXCUSES FOR HOUSEHOLD ISSUES

It's where the heart is. It's also where you first learn the fine art of excusing yourself for living like a slob.

➡ I ACTUALLY PREFER AN ECLECTIC LOOK

Not everyone can have a house that looks like it came straight out of *Metropolitan Home*. Basically, what you're saying here is that there is order to your disorder—that your lack of theme is in fact your theme. Fair enough. Just the fact that you've put a name to your decorating free-for-all ("eclectic") gives your style enough credibility that visitors will probably forgive you for your Nagel poster and beanbag chair. Although, for a Navajo print sofa, there is no redemption.

➡ I FOLLOWED THE RECIPE

The old saying may contend that "There's no accounting for taste." A newer saying might be "There's no use trying to account for a lack of taste."

➡ I JUST KEEP IT ON SO IT'S NOT SO QUIET AROUND HERE

When someone shows up at your door unannounced, and you've been rocking out to Radio Disney for the past few hours, you have to think fast.

➡ I MUST HAVE TAPED OVER IT

For a brief, shining moment, the medium of choice for preserving memories was the videocassette. And during that magical time, just about every family faced that tense moment when such treasured memories could not be found. The likely reason: Someone was scrambling at the last minute to record, say, the final episode of Melrose Place and accidentally grabbed the tape that should have been marked "Cody's Wedding."

➡ I'M DEFROSTING THE FRIDGE TOMORROW

Friends baffled as to why you've got nothing in your refrigerator except half a jar of mayo and a six of Bud? Of course, you've been clearing out everything in preparation for your semi-annual, oh-so-responsible defrosting. Stock up before your guest returns and you should be okay.

➡ I'M GOING TO TAKE CARE OF ALL OF THAT THIS WEEKEND

Ah, the weekend. That magical time in the not-so-distant future when there's all the time in the world to take care of all of the stored up dust on the floorboards, soap scum in the bathtub, grease on the stovetop, crumbs in the sofa, raw sewage in the basement. The beauty of it is that, even if you spend next weekend eating barbecued potato chips and watching ESPN, you can still use this excuse come Monday.

➡ IT HAS SENTIMENTAL VALUE

You can get away with having just about anything on display in your home—a driftwood sculpture, a square-dancing trophy, even a Hummel—if you have this excuse at the ready. After all, who can begrudge you a collection of State Fair commemorative thimbles if they know that they belonged to your beloved Aunt Tessa ... who rescued you from your evil stepparents and raised you as her own?

➡ IT'S USUALLY CLEANER THAN THIS

Okay, you are kind of stuck when someone you want to impress sees that the condition of your domicile is, shall we say, significantly less than sanitary. But this lame attempt doesn't really get you very far. Make sure that Visit Two is a dramatic improvement.

➡ MY LANDLORD SUCKS

One of the unheralded advantages of renting rather than owning is that you can blame your landlord for just about anything. This is especially useful when guests are turning their noses up at odd smells, shaking their heads at your pathetic flowerbeds, or jiggling the handle on the toilet.

➡ MY PARENTS BOUGHT IT FOR ME

A good explanation for awful artwork, awkward tchachkes, and strange books on your shelves. Not a good explanation for novelty underwear.

SOME ADDITIONAL EXCUSES FOR
HOUSEHOLD
ISSUES TO ADD TO YOUR REPERTOIRE

➤ **WE'VE TAKEN OUR DECORATING SCHEME FROM THE TRIBESPEOPLE OF NEW GUINEA.**

➤ **DIRT IS JUST MATTER THAT HASN'T FOUND ITS PLACE YET.**

➤ **CHEMICAL HOUSEHOLD CLEANERS ARE TERRIBLE FOR THE ENVIRONMENT.**

➤ **IT REALLY CAN BE CHEAPER TO EAT OUT EVERY NIGHT.**

➤ **I'M SAVING IT ALL FOR THE COMMUNITY GARAGE SALE.**

ICONIC EXCUSES

➡ BECAUSE IT'S THERE

Need an excuse to do something that is both a.) something nobody has done before and, b.) stupid?

Then this might be the line for you.

It was first uttered in March of 1923, when George Leigh Mallory, a British climber (not a climber of Brits—you know what I mean), was asked by a New York *Times* reporter why he had this burning desire to climb Mount Everest.

To give this some context, at 29,028 feet, is the highest point on Earth. At the time Mallory made his statement, nobody had made it to the top. Did he have a good excuse for risking his life and doing so? Nope. Just "Because it's there."

And so Mallory and his climbing buddy Andrew Irvine headed up the mountain.

Let's pause for a moment in the story to consider "Because it's there."

What the hell kind of an excuse is that?

While it might sound gutsy and macho coming from a mountain climber, it doesn't sound great coming from, say, an arsonist.

"Why did you burn down that convent?"

"Because it's there."

Or from the kid with the spray paint can.

"Why did you choose to decorate that bridge abutment with your gang sign?"

"Because it's, you know, there."

Our point is: Because it's there isn't really going to help you much. Unless you want to blow off a pesky New York Times reporter.

Now, when we last left Mallory, he was heading up the mountain—never to be seen alive again.

Sorry, we forgot to mention that part.

And it gets worse. In 1979, a Chinese climber named Wang Hongbao—who had even less reason to climb Everest, considering it had been conquered in 1953 by Edmund Hillary and Tenzing Norgay—reported finding a body. Unfortunately, Hongbao fell to his death the next day.

Hillary's body was finally found in 1999—only one of 179 people who have died while summiting Everest.

➡ BECAUSE THAT'S WHERE THEY KEEP THE MONEY

Before there was Slick Willie, the President of the United States, there was Slick Willie, the bank robber. Credited with holding up over 100 banks from the '20s to the '50s, Willie Sutton is also credited with one of the all time great excuses. The story goes that a reporter asked Sutton why he robs banks. His answer: "Because that's where they keep the money."

Unfortunately, according to Sutton's autobiography, he didn't say it. He claims the reporter made up the answer.

➡ WE NEEDED THE EGGS

The punch line of the classic joke, quoted in Woody Allen's Academy Award winner Annie Hall (Jeez, remember the days when Woody Allen was funny?). The joke goes something like this: Guy tells his doctor that his wife thinks she's a chicken. "How long has this been going on?" asks the doc. "About three years," says the guy. The doc asks, "Why didn't you come see me about this sooner?" The guy replies, "To tell you the truth, doc, we needed the eggs."

⇒ I GET IT FOR THE ARTICLES

Since *Playboy* magazine launched in 1955, lascivious readers have used the admittedly strong lineup of topnotch writers as an excuse to buy a magazine featuring exposed naughty bits.

And you know what? It's actually a pretty good excuse. *Playboy's* pages have been graced with work by John Steinbeck, John Updike, Tom Robbins, Alex Haley, Ray Bradbury, Truman Capote, Isaac Bashevis Singer and the list goes on and on. Its roster of contributors feels like a who's who of great writing of the last 50 or so years.

As Charles Taylor said in Slate magazine, "…when the history of American magazines is written, people who said 'I read it for the articles,' will have the last laugh." He then quotes Hugh Hefner, who once told a gathering of former Playmates, "Without you, I'd be the publisher of a literary magazine."

None of which explains why you're reading it in the bathroom.

➡ IT MUST BE LOST IN THE MAIL

"Where's the rent check?"

"Where's the alimony payment?"

"Did you ever send a gift?"

Well, the truth is, for whatever reason, you didn't.

Put the check in the mail. Send the gift. Whatever.

You just didn't. It might have sat there on the kitchen counter or on the dashboard of your car. Maybe you ran out of stamps or didn't bother really looking for them. Or maybe you didn't have the cash. Or you just plain forgot.

So what do you do?

Blame the mail service, of course.

And why not? When you find yourself backed into a corner, it's usually easiest to blame the biggest, most faceless entity you can find. And the U.S. Post Office is as big and as faceless an organization as there is.

Need proof of the faceless quality of this particular institution? Quick, which of the following was not a recent Postmaster General: John E. Potter, Christopher Richter, William J. Henderson, or Marvin T. Runyon?

We'll tell you a little later. If we told you right now, you'd have already glanced down while we was giving the choices. Admit it. That's what you would have done.

The point though, is that when you mention "postal employee," the image you get is a frustrated, sweaty guy with a shotgun. And no amount of PR has been about to change that.

Now, once you've decided to blame the post office, the question is: How effective is that diversion?

For that, we have to crunch some numbers.

U.S. figures are hard to come by (trust us—we asked Jeeves, visited ChaCha, and Googled until we were googly-eyed)—unless you go back to the Pony Express, which, in its 19 months of operation only lost mail twice. Pretty good.

In lieu of more contemporary American figures, we'll give you some Brit stats.

Royal Mail has openly stated that more than 14 million letters and parcels were lost, stolen, damaged or tampered with in 2005. Which seems like a ridiculous amount—until you consider that that's out of about 22 billion items.

If the U.S.—which handles about 212 billion pieces of mail a year, loses about the same percentage, then we set up our little equation like this:

$$\frac{14,000,000}{22,000,000,000} = \frac{x}{212,000,000,000}$$

Which comes out to about 135,000,000 pieces of mail lost each year.

We'd believe you if you told us that your piece of mail was one of them.

....

Oh, and Chris Richter was a college roommate. Not, at least so far, a Postmaster General of the United States.

EXCUSES FOR KIDS

When you're still in your formative years, you get a lot of leeway. Your parents—except in extreme extreme extreme circumstances—aren't going to kick you out. There's a lot you have to do to get kicked out of your school. And, chances are, your friends are going to be pretty forgiving. In fact, they are likely to think higher of you the more you get away with.

Of course, that doesn't mean that excuses are a cakewalk for the under-18 set. You can just be less stressed about using the right one knowing that one common denominator among all living people is that we were once younger than we are now.

AM I MY BROTHER'S KEEPER?

Say what you want about Cain, but you have to show a degree of respect for a guy who can throw a feeble excuse back … at the creator of the Universe. I mean, you know how hard it is to keep a straight face when you're BS-ing a parent or a teacher, imagine what this guy felt like trying to pull one over on the master of all things. And imagine the awed reaction a parent might get when this excuse is heard coming from the mouths of babes.

EVERYBODY DOES/IS DOING IT

There. You said it. If everyone was jumping off a bridge, you would too.

HE STARTED IT

A good sibling battle standby—although easily countered by "No, you started it," resulting in a stalemate.

I HAVE TOO MUCH HOMEWORK

When a kid is trying to get out of chores, this one will usually do the trick—making one seem diligent rather than just plain lazy. Of course, it helps if Mom and Dad don't hear the Xbox.

I LEARNED IT FROM YOU

Anyone over 35 should remember the public service TV commercial in which a dad catches his kids doing drugs and asks "Who taught you to do this?" and gets blasted with this reply. "Parents who do drugs have kids who do drugs" was the overt message. The subtler—and more useful one for the average person—is that if you can put the blame for your own actions squarely on the shoulders of your parents, you might get away with a shorter grounding.

➥ I'M JUST A KID. WHAT DO YOU EXPECT?

Young people get away with a tremendous amount of BS by planting the message that the accuser's standards were unrealistically high to begin with.

➥ THOSE AREN'T MY REAL PARENTS

When faced with "thinks-he's-hilarious" Dad and "has-to-tell-embarrassing-stories" Mom, kids of all ages will often drag out this never-believed excuse.

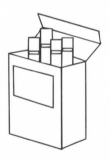

SOME ADDITIONAL EXCUSES FOR

 **KIDS**

TO ADD TO YOUR REPERTOIRE

➤ **ELMO TOLD ME TO.**

➤ **YOU'RE SHOWING YOUR AGE.**

➤ **THEY'RE CANDY CIGARETTES.**

➤ **WE WERE PRACTICING CPR.**

EXCUSES FOR
LATENESS

You walk a fine line when you try to explain away tardiness. On the one hand, you've left people hanging and insinuated that the people you left hanging have nothing better to do with their time than wait around for you. On the other hand, you tried your hardest to get there on time (you did try your hardest to get there on time, right), so you deserve some slack.

➡ I COULDN'T GET A CAB

The validity of some excuses depends on geography. Consider this one, which implies that 1.) The only way of getting to a place on time would be to take a cab, and 2.) It would have been reasonable for you to expect that the cab ride should have taken a significantly shorter amount of time. In other words, it's not going to fly in rural Tennessee.

Even in a big city, though, it can get a little dicey. Unless you are trying to depart from the New York theater district at curtain time, finding a cab shouldn't be too, too difficult. You might want to opt for There Was Unbelievable Traffic—or some combination of the two.

➡ I DON'T WEAR A WATCH

This feeble attempt at cooler-than-thou timelessness may sound slick to you, but to the rest of the world it just paints you as a self-absorbed idiot.

➡ I GOT BAD DIRECTIONS

In a Mapquest and Onstar world, it's harder and harder to get away with this old standby. And when you factor in the ubiquity of cell phones—with which you could have simply called for directions—well, the believability factor on this one is plummeting. Still, everyone's willing to believe that Mapquest has its glitches; so blaming it for a 15-minute delay is usually accepted without a blink.

Of course, you could up the hostility level by shifting to the variant You Gave Me the Wrong Directions, but be prepared for some push back if you can't come up with documentation.

➡ I HAD THE WRONG ADDRESS

A common lateness excuse that is rarely questioned. Asking someone why they had the wrong address seems ill-mannered—especially if the excusee is doing a nice job of acting harried and disappointed.

Now, if you can provide a name and description of the person who lives at the address that you claim to have inadvertently ended up at (and who answered the door when you knocked), then you, my friend, are golden.

➡ THERE WAS UNBELIEVABLE TRAFFIC

Similar to I Couldn't Get A Cab, this one is dependent on the understanding of area traffic patterns.

SOME ADDITIONAL
LATENESS
EXCUSES TO ADD TO YOUR REPERTOIRE

➤ TIME IS AN OUTDATED CONCEPT

➤ I HIT A DUCK

➤ I DIDN'T REALIZE IT WAS MORE IMPORTANT TO BE HERE THAN TO SAVE A BUSLOAD OF ORPHANS.

➤ DAMN CONVENTIONEERS, CLOGGING THE ROADS WITH THEIR PARADE.

➤ I HAD TO STOP DURING THE ECLIPSE. WHAT, YOU MISSED IT?

EXCUSES FOR LEAVING EARLY

You made an effort, right? You said you would show, and you showed. Now, it's time to move toward the nearest exit in an organized fashion. The trick is to get out the door without drawing too much attention to your departure—and perhaps even leave them wanting more.

➡ I CAN'T EAT SHELLFISH

People who can't tolerate crustaceans are serious about their food allergies. For them, a bucket of clams could mean a bucket of trouble, and we've all watched enough emergency room reality TV to know that a seizure is not a fun thing. No one will begrudge you for cutting out early on clambakes and crawfish boils.

➡ I'M FEELING A LITTLE QUEASY

Best to be as nonspecific as possible with this one. Provide too much information ("Must have been the crab dip"), and you open yourself up to cross-examination ("But we all had the crab dip, and no one else is feeling queasy.")

When it is delivered correctly, the beauty of this excuse is in its vaguely foreboding tone. While an amateur might go for the Academy Award, clutching his stomach and behaving as if he's one heave away from a Hot Zone situation, the true connoisseur knows to undersell this sudden state of affairs—the understanding being that the details of your situation are too unseemly to even discuss. So you'd best be leaving. Now!

➡ I'M GLUCOSE INTOLERANT

An allergy to wheat products gives you the perfect out for gatherings that turn into late-night pizza runs—because no one really wants to be a witness to your glucose-free version of late-night pizza runs.

➡ I'M LACTOSE INTOLERANT

Was there cream in that bolognaise? Did someone spike the guacamole with cheese? A sudden cramping feeling and the threat of monopolizing the bathroom is a perfectly good excuse for getting out of a social setting without too much protest, although it will probably threaten your status in the dinner party circuit. And the whole fondue craze will likely pass you by. Come to thing of it, that's not exactly a bad thing.

➡ MY DINNER ISN'T SITTING WELL

Give yourself about 20 minutes after eating, and then discreetly pull someone aside to say that things aren't going well in your lower GI region. You can briefly attribute your condition to a food allergy, a recent bout with the flu, or your stomach's unfamiliarity with butter-based French foods, but you needn't make a major announcement about it. Just tip off that one person, and let the social grapevine take care of the rest. If you don't get the sympathy vote, you can at least count on the empathy vote, because Lord knows we've all been there. Just one etiquette note: don't pull this at a dinner party, especially if you ever want the hostess to speak to you again.

➡ WE HAVE TO GET THE KIDS TO BED

Suffer the children. No one wants to think of your little ones padding around the house in their stocking feet, wondering when Mommy and Daddy are coming home from their kegger. Mention that you have bedtime story duty or that the babysitter needs to get home before her ankle band starts beeping, and you won't get pegged a party pooper. Do note, however, that you only have about a five-year window during which you can exploit your children in this way with any degree of credibility.

SOME ADDITIONAL
LEAVING EARLY
EXCUSES
TO ADD TO YOUR REPERTOIRE

➤ MY SPIDER SENSE IS TINGLING.

➤ I JUST REMEMBERED I HAVE A MEETING WITH MY PAROLE OFFICER.

➤ I CAN ONLY STAY IF YOU HAVE A PAIR OF BROWN TROUSERS I CAN CHANGE INTO ... IF YOU KNOW WHAT I MEAN.

➤ I'VE LIED AND NOW MY PANTS ARE ON FIRE.

EXCUSES FOR
LEGAL MATTERS

Most excuses come up when a social contact has been broken. Someone has an expectation of you that you haven't met, or you've made an agreement to do something that you haven't been able to fulfill.

But some excuses come up in circumstances where not social contracts, but actual on-the-books laws have been broken.

For those cases, we offer the following explanations, divided between those useful for minor infractions and those with more serious repercussions.

MINOR INFRACTIONS

➡ I DIDN'T REALIZE HOW FAST I WAS GOING

The lights appear in your rearview mirror and your mind starts working overtime. "My wife is in labor." (Of course, this will only work if there's a very pregnant woman in the car.) "I'm late to pick up my kids." (Similarly, best to actually have kids.) "The speed limit wasn't clearly posted." (Only an option if you are just a hair above what you know is the limit.) "I have diarrhea. Please. Please. Please let me get to a toilet." (A possibility, unless your officer is a bit of a sadist.) "My breaks weren't working" (Common, but not very solid—considering the officer will probably ask you to test your breaks.)

And then the officer approaches the car and, if you're smart, you utter, respectively, some variation of this one in answer to the cold, hard stare of the law.

Even if you do everything else right (pull over as quickly as is safe, have your license registration and insurance handy etc.), it's unlikely to get you out of the ticket. But it's also unlikely to make matters worse. Count your blessings.

➡ I HAVE BAD KNEES

Deep down, you know that handicap parking spots are reserved for people with certifiable limitations. Even if you can pull off a really good limp, using these "handy" slots as a convenience for those times when you just don't feel like walking the extra 15 yards to the Wal-Mart entrance is not going to endear you to anyone. Not the traffic cop, not your fellow law-abiding shoppers, and not the double amputee who had to wheel himself all the way in from employee parking because you took his spot. And that's not even factoring in the bad juju.

⇒ I WAS ONLY GOING TO BE IN THE STORE FOR A MINUTE

To you, parking in the fire lane while you run in to buy your Powerball ticket might seem like the essence of efficiency, but that reasoning isn't going to fly with the officer who is slipping the parking ticket under your wiper blade. Telling him that you'll share your millions with him probably won't win you any points either.

⇒ IT'S A VICTIMLESS CRIME

A victimless crime is one where a case can be made that no one is harmed. Everything from flag desecration to participating in your office Final Four pool to offering an unlicensed fireworks display to bigamy gets lumped in here, along with drug use, prostitution, adultery, obscenity or driving without a seat belt. And cloning. Can't forget cloning.

You can quibble about the victimlessness of any of these, but that doesn't get around the fact that, in the eyes of the law, you don't need a victim for an act to be criminal. Still, if it helps you get through the first few nights in your cell, just keep saying it to yourself.

⇒ IT'S NO MORE A DRUG THAN CAFFEINE

Yeah, but caffeine has a little bonus: It's not against the law.

➡ IT'S UNCOMFORTABLE

From overweight people in seatbelts to kids having to wear ties to just about any guy trying to get out of using a condom, discomfort is a common attempt to get out of things expected of you. The reality, though, is that the car that hits you isn't concerned about your comfort. Neither is your mother dressing you, or your justifiably concerned partner.

➡ THE LIGHT WAS YELLOW

Unfortunately, by the time you get to the point of making this excuse, it's probably too late for any sort of excuse.

➡ MATHEMATICAL ERROR

Blaming math for an error is like blaming a hammer for hitting your finger. Still, since few adults remember anything beyond eighth grade arithmetic, this excuse gets accepted far more often than it statistically should. Except, of course, when filing your taxes.

➡ THE METER WAS BROKEN

The problem is, unless you intend to break it before the ticket-writer shows up, it's going to be pretty obvious that it's working.

MAJOR INFRACTIONS

➠ GOD TOLD ME TO

No matter what your religious persuasion, do you really expect us to believe that the Maker of All Things has chosen you as a prophet?

➠ HE WAS ALWAYS QUIET AND NEVER ANY TROUBLE

Ah, the tough life of the serial killer's neighbor. What to say when the reporters are hounding you for quotes because they have no other information to fill their airtime? This is a convenient go-to statement that absolves you of involvement but also makes you come across as clueless. (Especially when the sound of a chainsaw at odd hours of the night should have clued you in.)

➠ HE/SHE WAS ASKING FOR IT

Maybe so. But you'd better have it in writing.

➠ I ACTED IN SELF-DEFENSE

Usually a good claim to make if a witness and/or DNA evidence isn't involved. It also helps if you are significantly lighter and/or older than the corpse in question.

➡ I CAME FROM A BROKEN HOME

Whether you arose from Dickensian circumstance or you simply broke a thing or two around your childhood home, blaming the past has a tried and true history of weaseling out of things in the present.

➡ I DIDN'T KNOW IT WAS LOADED

There are some excuses that there simply aren't any excuses for. This is one of them.

➡ I HAD A LOUSY LAWYER

Forget how bad your case was—or the (alleged) fact that you actually committed the crime in question: When all else fails (in other words, when you hear the word "guilty" without first hearing the word "not"), you can always try this one. It may not get you a retrial, but it could be a good icebreaker when trying to get to know your new cellmate.

➡ I SAW IT IN A MOVIE/TV SHOW

There's a very good reason why "don't try this at home" has become a cliché in the movies and television: Because since nearly the beginning of the industry, people have pointed to the screen as an excuse for their crimes.

White Heat, A Clockwork Orange, Magnum Force, The Deer Hunter, The Matrix, Robocop, Natural Born Killers, and most notoriously, Taxi Driver, all had fingers pointed at them.

It's not just guys with guns who credit the cinema with inspiration. Jackass—first on the small screen, then on the large—has inspired a generation of, well, jackasses to kayak down stairs and spray themselves with fire extinguishers.

So why not jump on the bandwagon yourself?

One good reason: People who do what people in the movies and on TV do are pretty much universally seen as idiots. That includes not only those who copy violent acts, but also anybody who copied the fashions of Sex in the City, thought saying "Heyyyyyy" like Fonzie from Happy Days would make them cool, or bought a piece of jewelry "inspired" by Titanic.

➡ I'M A MINOR

If you are under 10 years old, this one might hold water. If that's the case, just about anything you do falls under the doli incapax rule, which keeps you from being held legally responsible for your actions. When you're between the ages of 10 and 18, though, things get a little fuzzier. Yes, you are a minor in most places if you are under 18, but you might not be a juvenile when it comes to having to take the heat for your actions. In some states, the cutoff is 16. In others, 17.

Still, it's worth a shot … err, a try.

➡ I'M INNOCENT BY REASON OF INSANITY

First, let's get straight what is being said when a lawyer presents this one. A person is not responsible for his or her criminal conduct if, at the time of the offense, he or she had a severe enough mental disease or defect that he or she could not understand the nature of the offense. That's slightly different from the common usage where the definition is something like this: A person is innocent by reason of insanity if he or she can't figure any other way out of getting thrown in jail.

➡ I'M JUST DOING THE WORK THAT NOBODY ELSE WILL

Sorry. Whether you're Dirty Harry, Curtis Sliwa, or Batman, you're still going to have to see how your attempts to rid the streets of bad guys match up against the laws of the land.

➡ IT'S LEGAL

In theory, laws are not synonymous with morality. Only a handful of the Ten Commandments, for example, are really illegal (although coveting your neighbor's wife too obviously could result in you getting your clock cleaned.) Therefore ipso facto ergo sum (or something like that), just because something is legal doesn't make it okay. Nice try.

➡ IT'S LEGAL IN CANADA

Whether it involves the unauthorized sharing of music downloads, medicinal marijuana or going topless in public, claiming that the law you're breaking is not an issue in Canada doesn't take the edge off your crime—nor does it make you seem particularly worldly.

➡ IT SHOULD BE LEGAL

Unfortunately, the arresting officer standing over you as you wipe off the molasses and chicken feathers is unlikely to be terribly interested in your political position.

➡ POLICE BRUTALITY

It happens. We know that. But pulling this excuse out without merit sets you up for some very, very bad karma.

SOME ADDITIONAL

LEGAL
EXCUSES

TO ADD TO YOUR REPERTOIRE

➤ **FORGERY? BUT I ONLY DID IT THREE TIMES, NOT FOUR.**

➤ **SO WHAT? I HAVE A GET OUT OF JAIL FREE CARD.**

➤ **PREMEDITATED? I'VE NEVER MEDITATED IN MY ENTIRE LIFE.**

➤ **WHAT MAKES YOU THINK YOUR COURT IS SO SUPREME?**

➤ **DEITIES ARE ABOVE THE LAW.**

➤ **THIS IS PERFORMANCE ART.**

MEDICAL EXCUSES

In an ideal world, we would not have to make excuses for physical problems. In an ideal world, we would take good care of our bodies. In an ideal world, this book would probably not exist.

➡ EXHAUSTION

This excuse would be perfectly believable if it were uttered by a fire-fighter, a mineworker, a soldier or field hands. The problem is, you never hear it in regard to firefighters, mineworkers, solders or field hands. You hear it from Mariah Carey and Lindsay Lohan. Or, at least, from their publicists, who are no doubt pretty exhausted themselves.

➡ FEMALE TROUBLE

Yes, there are times when, for many women, certain times of the month can lead to mood swings and—to put it gently—testiness. And it's nice to have a line that will get you out of any unfriendly behavior after the fact.

The problem is, once you use this as an excuse for your behavior, you leave others open to using it as an excuse for just about anything you do. Worse, it reinforces the sexist notion that women are at the mercy of biology. The extreme extension of this idea is the bozos who think that the U.S. shouldn't have a female president because of the increased risk of her doing something irrationally, Earth-shatteringly drastic every couple of weeks.

Ridiculous, yes. But do you really want to aid such thinking, even in a small way?

➡ THE GERBIL MUST HAVE CRAWLED UP THERE ALL BY ITSELF

No need to comment further.

➡ I FLOSS EVERY DAY

No, you don't.

But that's what you say to the dental hygienist as she takes care of your annual cleaning. Wasted effort, though. Not the flossing, the insisting that you do floss. Because who better to know the truth than the person removing six months' worth of popcorn hulls and Jujubee reside from your gum line?

And while you promise yourself you'll do better, you know you won't. Even though you know it's good for you. Even though such notables as Julia Roberts, Natalie Merchant, Homer Simpson and Broom Hilda can be found on flossing.org, the website of the National Flossing Council, doing the string thing (okay, so Julia was in character—in Pretty Woman). Even though flossing not only keeps your teeth healthy, it also saved the life of Terry Watson, a sailor who, while missing at sea for two months in 2002, managed to temporarily repair his ship's sail using, yes, you guessed it.

➡ I THINK I HAVE THE FLU

We've all had it, which is why we all assume a "Better you than me, Buddy" attitude when we hear about someone having to stay home, close to the Vicks salve and Kleenex. (Double that sentiment if we're talking about stomach flu.)

However, this universal pardon is beginning to show signs of overuse. If you're going to play the influenza card, you'd better be able to back it up with a fever and some actual mucus.

➡ I THINK I'VE GOT FOOD POISONING

Yes, there are true cases of food poisoning reported every day. But breakfast, lunch and dinner would be the most dangerous times of day if there were actual contamination to back up every case of food poisoning reported by a hung-over employee to a gullible employer.

Still, because the news media reports the real cases on a reasonably regular basis, food poisoning is a call-in-sick excuse that isn't as seasonal as I Think I Have the Flu and far more easy to dismiss the next day when you return to work.

➡ I'M A CHRISTIAN SCIENTIST

This excuse may help you get out of a visit to the doctor—since practitioners believe that the non-reality of illness can be conquered in other ways. But to be consistent, you should read up on Mary Baker Eddy and start referring to God as "the Father-Mother."

➡ I'M ALLERGIC TO CATS

By some estimates, approximately 2 percent of the United States population is allergic to cats, so you have a lot of leeway with this pardon. The watery eyes and itchy nose will get you a little bit of sympathy, along with the likely suggestion that you should just take some Benadryl and tough it out. But when the coughing, wheezing, shortness of breath, and hard-to-ignore death rattle kick in, your host will almost certainly put the catnip ball down long enough to show you to the door.

➡ I'M NOT SURE WHAT IT IS, BUT I WON'T GET THE TESTS BACK UNTIL TUESDAY

Mysterious illnesses are always good. And suggesting that you've called in the big guns not only gives you absolution (because clearly you're working on a cure), but also adds a bit of cache—as if you might someday be the inspiration for a JAMA article.

➡ IT'S MY ALLERGIES

This generic plea only works as a getaway plan if you are showing actual physical symptoms. Unless you're sneezing, vomiting, or bleeding from the ears, people will assume that you're simply allergic to having a life.

➡ IT'S MY ASTHMA

Because the symptoms of asthma can range from mild to life threatening, this excuse works a lot of times because it is so shrouded in uncertainty. When you pull this one out of the health-issue hat, you could be saying that you're feeling a little short of breath, or you could be announcing to the party that you're one gasp away from needing your EpiPen.

➡ IT'S THE NURSE'S/INTERN'S/ RESIDENT'S FAULT

Sorry, Dr. Centeroftheuniverse, these are the people who cover for you every day. Nobody's buying it.

MEDICAL EXCUSES

THAT MIGHT BE WORTH A SHOT

➤ I'VE GOT
A.) BODYBUILDERS PSYCHOSIS,
B.) CASINO FEET,
C.) HOLIDAY DEPRESSION,
D.) FRISBEE FINGER,
E.) JOYSTICK DIGIT
(ALL ACTUAL CONDITIONS, BELIEVE IT OR NOT).

➤ BUT IT WORKED ON E.R.

➤ I'M NOT A DOCTOR, BUT I PLAYED ONE IN MY BACK YARD.

➤ SELF-SURGERY IS THE WAY OF THE FUTURE.

➤ WELL, DOC, IT'S BECAUSE I'VE GOT A BAD CASE OF LOVIN' YOU.

ODIFEROUS EXCUSES

There are few situations in life that are as embarrassing as knowing that the answer to the question, "What's that smell?" is you. Ignorance and denial will only get you so far. When there's no way around fessing up to a stink, all you can do is cross your fingers and hope that one of these Hail Mary excuses flies.

➥ HE THAT SMELT IT, DEALT IT

A classic diversionary technique that, in essence, points blame at the messenger. The more colloquial version, The Smeller's the Feller, works just as well.

➥ I COULDN'T HOLD IT IN/BETTER OUT THAN IN

Less of an excuse and more of a statement of the obvious.

➥ I MUST HAVE STEPPED IN SOMETHING

Maybe you really did track something in on the sole of your shoe. Or, maybe you simply let something rip, and man's best friend is (yet again) covering for you. (See also: It Must Have Been the Dog, The Dog Ate My Homework, Hair of the Dog.)

➥ I'M LACTOSE INTOLERANT

Another good excuse for accidentally calling an audible, gastronomically speaking. Having a bottle of Lactaid on hand helps reinforce this one.

➥ I'M TRYING A NEW DEODORANT

You'd be surprised how well this excuse works in those humiliating moments when you lift your arm, and the room suddenly smells like cumin. People feel your pain, and you can tell by the way their faces are all scrunched up.

Nobody should blame you for trying something new. After all, it takes a little experimentation to figure out if you're an Arid Extra Dry guy or a Lady Speed Stick—and it is a fact of science that sometimes experiments go horribly wrong. Just don't try to use this excuse two days in a row

➡ IN MANY CULTURES, THAT'S A COMPLIMENT

Of course, it would be helpful if you could actually name some of those cultures.

➡ IT MUST HAVE BEEN THE DOG

Gas is passed. If the room consists entirely of men and it is a man doing the gassing, then credit is usually taken.

If, however, the company is mixed (or if a woman is doing the gassing), then chances are that credit is not taken. And if the odor is particularly odorous or if the volume is particularly loud, then an excuse must appear quickly.

The presence of a canine is useful in such situations. Flatulence in dogs is a well-documented issue, popularized in the bluntly named children's book *Walter the Farting Dog*. Besides, could there possibly be a better fall guy than man's best friend?

SOME ADDITIONAL
ODIFEROUS
EXCUSES
TO ADD TO YOUR REPERTOIRE

➤ IN OLDEN TIMES (THE RENAISSANCE? THE REFORMATION? WHAT DO I LOOK LIKE, A HISTORY BOOK?), A BATH ONCE A MONTH WAS THE NORM.

➤ NO, WHAT IT SMELLS LIKE IS TEEN SPIRIT.

➤ IF IT WILL HELP EASE SOMEONE'S EMBARRASSMENT, I'LL TAKE THE BLAME FOR THAT ONE.

➤ **THE PERFUME INDUSTRY HAS RUINED THINGS FOR EVERYBODY.**

➤ **COME ON, IT'S FUNNY. BREAKING WIND IS ALWAYS FUNNY.**

➤ **EVERYONE SMELLS THIS WAY IN EUROPE.**

EXCUSES FOR
OVEREATING/ NOT EXERCISING

In Dante's *Inferno*, there was a special ring of hell for folks with a tendency to overindulge on food and drink. If the *Divine Comedy* were written in modern day, there might also be an area set aside for everyone who had an unused health club membership.

So maybe you don't eat like Jenny Craig or exercise like Rocky Balboa. You have your reasons. We've listed some of them here.

➡ I DIDN'T WANT IT TO GO BAD

Some people say that their body is a temple. What you're saying when you use this excuse for polishing off half a carton of chocolate milk is that your body is a temple that accepts all kinds.

➡ I HAD A TWO-FOR-ONE

Like its cousin I Had a Coupon over in the retail section, this cheapskate excuse only gets you so far. If it means having a discount lunch with a friend and splitting the tab, that's one thing. If it means dining solo and consuming two Big Buford sandwiches instead of one, that's quite another.

➡ I HAVE THE MUNCHIES

Somewhere, somehow, we came to believe that "munching" was something inherently different from "eating." Oh, that it were so. As it is, "excessive munching" doesn't sound nearly as bad as "overeating," but it has the same effect. Magnifying the lameness of this excuse is the fact that almost everyone is familiar with nutrition's new math. One serving of Wheat Thins, for example, contains 6 grams of fat while a serving of lean pork tenderloin has 4 grams. In other words, no one's going to think of you as a dainty eater if you keep a running inventory of what's in the office vending machine.

➡ I JUST DON'T HAVE TIME TO EXERCISE

Need all-inclusive coverage to explain the tire around your gut? For generations, the low number of hours in the day have been blamed for the high number of cottage cheese dimples on a person's upper thigh.

But while such an excuse is common, that doesn't make it supportable. Simply calculating the number of hours spent watching TV or trolling the Internet is usually enough to invalidate the "no time" statement.

➡ I SKIPPED LUNCH

That may well be, but it's not really justification for pulling your chair up to the buffet. And the skipped lunch excuse only works if you've also skipped your mid-morning snack, your post-lunch nibble, your mid-afternoon bite, and your pre-dinner treat.

➡ I WAS NERVOUS

How, your roommate wants to know, did that fresh supply of Oreos suddenly transform into a few black and white crumbs at the bottom of a crinkly package? Yes, Munchie McBinger, you ate the whole package … and trying to divert attention from the selfish reality to a poor pity me pose is unlikely to generate much sympathy from your hungry friend.

➡ I'M BIG-BONED

Or maybe, just maybe, you've eaten too many barbecued ribs.

➡ I'M JUST BLOATED

There is a long list of situations that could lead to abdominal bloating or swelling. Among them are food allergies, hernia, and appendicitis.

No shame in any of those.

But a burgeoning belly leads the curious to other conclusions—the two principal ones being that you're pregnant and that you're just getting fatter. And, if either of those are the case, no amount of restating that you are bloated is going to convince anyone. Besides, the truth will come out shortly anyway, when those extra inches around the waist don't go away.

➡ IT'S MY METABOLISM

Unfortunately, it's difficult to blame your metabolism for taking a fourth trip to the dessert cart.

➡ THESE ARE MY SKINNY JEANS

To the rest of the world, the muffin top spilling over the waistband of your Levi 501s, and the fact that you could bounce a quarter on your denim-encased butt are signs that you need to trade in your jeans for something a size (or two, or three) up. To you, however, the fact that you can even contain your flesh inside this particular article of clothing is a victory. Unfortunately, the phrase isn't "Close only counts in horse-shoes, hand grenades, and size 4 jeans," which means that stretching the limits of fabric in such a self-congratulatory way doesn't give you the air of someone who's "still got it," but rather as someone who's let herself go.

➡ THEY'RE LOW-FAT

Fine, but the understanding is that you are eating those low-fat foods in the recommended serving size and not by the box or bag.

➡ THEY WERE STUCK TOGETHER

Someone brings a coffee cake to work. That coffee cake is sliced into enough pieces to feed the entire office, which means each piece is the approximate size of a matchbook. Now, what if the knife didn't go all the way through? What if you touched both your piece of the coffee cake and the two adjoining pieces? You'd have to take the entire trio, right? It might not make you employee of the month, but at least you'd get enough coffee cake to hold you over until you can get your next bag of Doritos from the vending machine.

This excuse also works well with pizza and tater tots.

SOME ADDITIONAL EXCUSES FOR
OVEREATING/
NOT EXERCISING
TO ADD TO YOUR REPERTOIRE

➤ MY GYM WAS CONDEMNED.

➤ I BOUGHT MY EQUIPMENT FROM AN INFOMERCIAL AND I'M NOT SUPPOSED TO EXERCISE AGAIN UNTIL THE TRIAL.

➤ THEY HAVE CAMERAS AT THE GYM AND THE PICTURES END UP ON THE INTERNET.

➤ I HATE RICHARD SIMMONS.

EXCUSES FOR PARENTS

Nobody said being a parent was going to be easy. And nobody said that being a parent means you suddenly have a cache of excuses that are any better than the ones you had before you added another being to the world's population.

➡ BECAUSE I'M YOUR MOTHER, THAT'S WHY

And clearly you couldn't think of anything even close to a decent excuse.

➡ HE JUST FELL IN WITH THE WRONG CROWD

It isn't your kid's fault he's a juvenile delinquent. It's those kids he's been hanging around with.

And in a related matter, where could your dear child have possibly learned how to dodge responsibility?

➡ I DON'T KNOW WHAT THEY'RE TEACHING HER IN THAT SCHOOL

Well, maybe you should try going to a Back to School night one of these years and find out what they're teaching her.

But that's not really the point of this excuse. The point is to shift blame from you to the teachers at your kids' school. After all, your kids spend a lot more time there than they do at home. And when you take away the time they spend in front of their computer, at their game console, watching TV, and doing god-knows-what behind the locked door of their bedrooms … er, never mind.

➡ I'M DOING THIS FOR YOUR OWN GOOD

Once the go-to excuse for handing out an old-fashioned ass-whoopin', this excuse is now used by parents everywhere for doing just about anything that their kids don't like.

➧ IT'S NO USE. HE WON'T LISTEN TO ME

An effective—if overused—way for a parent to avoid doing actual parenting, this statement signifies that the parent in question has officially given up.

➧ THAT'S HOW I WAS BROUGHT UP

If that's a reason for action, then why don't you willingly accept $2.50 an hour salary, watch lame detective shows like Mannix and listen to The Village People without irony?

➧ YOU'RE SUPPOSED TO HONOR YOUR MOTHER AND FATHER

This one might hold up if you and the young 'uns are actually respecting the rest of the commandments. Then again, you have to understand why your kids have a tough time honoring you when you listen to the kind of music you do. And what is that thing you're wearing?

SOME ADDITIONAL

PARENTING
EXCUSES

TO ADD TO YOUR REPERTOIRE

➤➤ **THAT KID? NEVER SAW HIM BEFORE.**

➤➤ **RITALIN? CHEWABLE VITAMINS? THEY'RE EASY TO MIX UP.**

➤➤ **THAT TRAIT MUST HAVE SKIPPED A GENERATION.**

➤➤ **HE LOVES CARS—THAT'S WHY I LET HIM SIT OUT HERE IN THE PARKING LOT WHILE I VISIT THE CASINO.**

EXCUSES FOR
PARTYING HARD

In this great big world of ours, there are lots of reasons to celebrate. There's weddings. There's birthdays. There's anniversaries. There's Fridays.

Excuses often pop up the next day (preferably, not too early), when we hazily look back on our activities and desperately try to explain them away. But sometimes we also get challenged while we are in the act of partying—usually by some stick in the mud who is JUST NO FUN!!!

➥ HAIR OF THE DOG

With some seasoned partiers, the perfect morning remedy for a hangover comes in liquid form. As in Bloody Mary's, Mimosas, and Irish coffees. "Hair of the dog" is short for the phrase "hair of the dog that bit you," which paraphrases the Scottish fable "If this dog do you bite, soon as out of your bed, take a hair of the tail in the morning." The theory is that having a little more of the substance that is making you feel ill will lessen, or at least prolong, the impending symptoms of withdrawal. Some people swear by this particular … um … homeopathic remedy. If you hoist your can of Bud any time after lunch, though, people will know you're just using it as an excuse for going on a two-day bender.

➥ I'M CELEBRATING

As mentioned in the introduction, there's no shortage of reasons to celebrate. Of course, the further the celebration seems to be from the spirit of the event being celebrated, the more trouble you are going to have with this excuse. In other words, we don't recommend a round of bar-hopping to commemorate the completion of your DUI-inspired community service sentence.

➥ IT'S NOT HURTING ANYBODY BUT MYSELF

In certain circles, the pathetic undertones of this statement will work to your advantage. In so many words, you're announcing that you take full responsibility for your self-destructive behavior and the inevitable consequences. Be warned, however, that making such a bold statement also implies that you're not going to require babysitting later on (in the form of someone to pay for your cab fare home or bail you out of jail in the morning.)

➡ IT'S SPRING BREAK

From a cold sore to an extended appearance in a Girls Gone Wild! DVD, embarrassing and unwanted side effects of spring break are many. Rationalizations, on the other hand, are few.

➡ IT'S TRADITION

You might get a pass if the drinking tradition you are referring to comes from, say, the Talmud, which instructs that a "person is obligated to drink on Purim until he does not know the difference between 'cursed be Haman' and 'blessed be Mordechai (that's a serious binge when can't tell the bad guy from the good guy in the Book of Esther). This excuse might not be so readily accepted, though, if the tradition you are referring to involves a video camera, a ladder and shots of Jagermeister, and was started last weekend by your fraternity brother.

➡ JESUS DRANK WINE

True, oh Biblical scholar. But he didn't sleep on the curb while his buddies tried to remember all the verses to American Pie.

➡ YOU'RE ONLY YOUNG ONCE

Depending on your definition of "once," this is technically correct. However, it's only half a statement. The other half could just as easily be "therefore you should try to be in control of your senses during that oh-so-short time."

SOME ADDITIONAL
PARTYING
EXCUSES
TO ADD TO YOUR REPERTOIRE

➤➤ REMEMBER THE Y2K THING?
THEY WERE OFF BY A COUPLE OF YEARS.

➤➤ I PARTY THEREFORE I AM!

- **MY FAVORITE ROLLER DERBY TEAM MADE THE LEAGUE SEMI-FINALS!**

- **ANOTHER JUDE LAW MOVIE HAS BEEN RELEASED!**

- **IT'S TALK LIKE A PIRATE DAY!**

- **WHEW! I GOT MY PERIOD!**

PERSONAL RELATIONSHIP
·····EXCUSES·····

Love may make the world go 'round, but things get difficult if the one who wants to go around the world with you isn't someone you want to go around the world with. Or vice versa.

Sometimes, this knowledge happens before there's even a first date, leading to one set of excuses. Sometimes, it happens much later, leading to another. In the middle, there's plenty of room for variation. Through it all, some common excuses arise.

➡ I DON'T LIKE YOU IN THAT WAY

After your best buddy takes that awkward stab at a kiss, this is the standard line. Expect it to be followed by some awkward silence, a few minutes of random conversation that neither of you is really listening to, and then, as soon as possible, a sprint for the door. The prospect of salvaging your friendship will be increased slightly if your next few encounters occur within large groups. Provided, of course, that the rest of the group isn't coupled off.

➡ I JUST HAD A REALLY BAD BREAKUP AND I'M TAKING SOME TIME OFF

While it is universally understood that the "time off" you are taking will end as soon as you meet someone really hot, using this line does help the rejected party live briefly in the illusion that the rejection he or she just suffered would have happened to anyone.

➡ I LOST YOUR NUMBER

I know. I know. You didn't expect to bump into him again and you want to put him down gently. 'Tis a noble thing. And certainly gentler than the truth, which is likely something like "Giving me your number was the biggest waste of paper since Vanna White published her autobiography."

➡ I NEED TO CHECK MY CALENDAR

When you don't want to make a commitment on the spot—and hope to come up with a better excuse later—this is a standard interim move. Bonus points because it's nearly impossible to argue with—unless you happen to be holding your palm pilot at the time.

➥ I WAS IN LOVE

"But love is blind," said Jessica in Shakespeare's *The Merchant of Venice*—as have millions of people since as they watched otherwise smart people turn themselves into candidates for The Jerry Springer Show. As an excuse, "I Was in Love" holds up a lot better than "But I love him/her?" because it implies that time has brought some wisdom and that the same mistakes are less likely to be committed again (at least in the same form or with the same person).

➥ I'M SEEING SOMEONE

The less you know the person hitting on you, the better the chance of pulling this off. If you need specifics without having to produce evidence, you can always call on the I Have a Girlfriend/Boyfriend in Canada variation.

➥ IT'S BEST FOR THE KIDS

Till death do you part? Well, maybe not.

Sure there are circumstances. And the differences may truly be irreconcilable. But your kids are likely to feel even more confused if you try to convince them that your split-up is the best thing that could happen to them.

➡ IT'S NOT YOU, IT'S ME

Hey, we get it. You don't want the person you are breaking up with to feel like he or she has done anything wrong. You're trying to minimize the collateral damage. Bully for you.

But before you think that this excuse puts you in line for sainthood, think again. As well-intentioned—and as sincere—as you may feel you are being as you rehearse this statement, know in advance that it rarely comes across as anything more than a cliché.

A side note for guys: When objects are hurled at you, guard your face and privates and get out of the room as quickly as possible.

A side note for gals: Prepare for him to use your guilt to get one last roll in the hay with you … before telling his friends what a bitch you are.

➡ YOU'RE JUST NOT MY TYPE

Ah, the wonderful vagueness of "my type." It allows you to bail on anyone without any sort of explanation.

PERSONAL
RELATIONSHIP

EXCUSES TO ADD TO YOUR REPERTOIRE

➤ I JUST FOUND OUT WE'RE COUSINS.

➤ I HAVE THIS IRRATIONAL FEAR OF ANYONE
WITH AN EXCEPTIONALLY LARGE FOREHEAD.

➤ I JUST FOUND OUT THE POST OFFICE DIDN'T
LOSE MY MAIL-ORDER BRIDE.

➤ I JUST HAVE YOUR ROOMMATE'S CELL PHONE NUM-
BER ON MY SPEED DIAL IN CASE OF EMERGENCY.

➤ OF COURSE I LOVE YOU. I JUST SAVE MY MYSPACE
TOP EIGHT FOR, YOU KNOW, PEOPLE WHO
WOULD GET UPSET IF THEY WEREN'T IN THERE.

POLITICAL
· · · · · · · · EXCUSES· · · · · · · ·

Imagine having to come up with an excuse for your actions when there are dozens of people watching you.

Now add a half dozen or so zeroes to that number and you'll start to get an idea of the position politicians can find themselves in when there's some explaining to do.

➡ BIG GOVERNMENT

Want to know what's wrong with just about anything in the country? Ask any non-incumbent candidate for public office and he or she will tell you this.

Are they right? Part of the time. Problem is, it's difficult to tell which part.

➡ I AM NOT A CROOK

In a televised Q and A with the Associated Press on November 17, 1973, President Richard M. Nixon dealt with numerous accusations of wrongdoing with the statement "…people have got to know whether or not their President's a crook. Well, I am not a crook."

Not only did he create one of the most memorable presidential quotes since "Fourscore and seven years ago," he also coined one of the best examples of the straight-up denial excuse. And he gave '70s impressionist Rich Little a major career boost.

What he was doing was making use of a not-quite-an-excuse distraction. The process is simple: After an accusation is made, put words into the mouth of the accuser, and then deny the simplified allegation. Stay as non-specific as possible.

Example:

Your sister says that you borrowed a sweater without asking.

She: Did you take my sweater without asking?

You: Are you calling me a thief? I am not a thief.

See how easy, if not presidential, that is?

Of course, things didn't work out too well for Tricky Dick, so take that into account when you try this one yourself.

➡ I DID NOT HAVE SEX WITH THAT WOMAN

Another classic in the realm of real-life political excuses (See also I Am Not A Crook,). We don't recommend quibbling over definitions when two elements are involved: a.) the mass media, and b.) pants around ankles.

➡ I DON'T LIKE ANY OF THE CANDIDATES

Join the crowd, pal.

➡ IT'S NECESSARY FOR NATIONAL SECURITY

There are, to be fair, many, many things that may well be necessary for our national security. But this excuse can also be used as a reason to do just about anything, Constitutional or not.

➡ MY OPPONENT STARTED THE NEGATIVE CAMPAIGNING

Always, always, always claim that the other candidate started it. That way, you can say just about anything you want about the lying, cheating, fornicating, backstabbing, money laundering lout who clearly has loyalties with a foreign government and bent on robbing senior citizens of their hard-earned social security money.

➡ MY VOTE DOESN'T MATTER

Statistically, you're probably right. It is extremely unlikely, even if you vote in every possible election in your lifetime, that your vote will make the difference in an election. And, sometimes, there's not a logical answer for why you should do something. So, at the risk of sounding like your high school civics teacher, we are going to resort to this: If you can't muster the energy to get off your ass and vote, then you don't deserve to complain.

Of course, your political life shouldn't begin and end in the polling booth, but that's another matter.

➡ PARTISAN GRIDLOCK

Can't get your pork bill passed? Blame the two-party system, which is designed, in part, to keep legislation such as your pork bill from passing.

➡ THE WEATHER KEPT PEOPLE AWAY FROM THE POLLS

The question, of course, is how loyal were voters who were afraid of that dreaded thing known as … precipitation.

➡ WEAPONS OF MASS DESTRUCTION

It may have been a good enough excuse to start one costly and deadly war, but it probably won't work a second time.

POLITICAL EXCUSES

TO ADD TO YOUR REPERTOIRE

➤ WHAT DO I KNOW? I'M FROM A PURPLE STATE.

➤ THE HARDING ADMINISTRATION SOURED ME ON POLITICS.

➤ I DIDN'T MAKE IT TO THE POLLS BECAUSE MY CHAD WAS HANGING.

➤ I BELIEVE IN A THREE-PARTY SYSTEM—AND HAVING GONE TO THREE PARTIES THE NIGHT BEFORE THE ELECTION, I COULDN'T GET UP IN THE MORNING.

➤ OKAY, SO MAYBE HE DIDN'T WIN. BUT I VOTED FOR HIM TO PLACE. OR WAS IT SHOW?

➤ THAT'S JUST THE KIND OF THING I WOULD EXPECT FROM SOMEONE WHO HAS BEEN CO-OPTED BY AN UNSUSTAINABLE POLITICAL SYSTEM.

➤ I'M PART KENNEDY.

RANDOM
·······EXCUSES·······

So many excuses. So little time. Here's is a quick rundown of time-tested excuses that don't fit into any of the above categories but, none-theless, are good to have around.

➡ BUT I SAW THE MOVIE

So did a few million other people. We're asking you about the book.

➡ BUT I SENT YOU AN INVITATION

No, you didn't. But when that friend or family member who didn't make your cut gets wind of your soiree, there's little to do but pretend he or she did.

➡ HE WAS ASKING FOR IT

A favorite comebacks of neighborhood bullies everywhere, this one posits the notion that one might actually request a fat lip or bloody nose.

➡ HOW DID THAT GET THERE?

Assuming total cluelessness sometimes actually works. Of course, when you're high and your stash has been found, sometimes it only seems to work.

➡ I DON'T HAVE ANY CLEAN CLOTHES

It's rarely a good idea to drag out an excuse that makes you sound like you live in your own filth.

➡ I HAVEN'T HAD MY COFFEE

Being zoned out in the morning becomes a little easier to understand when you mumble this one.

➡ I HEARD IT FROM A RELIABLE SOURCE

Unnamed sources are the bread and butter of an investigative journalist. Unfortunately, you're not an investigative journalist. You're just a person spreading a nasty, unfounded rumor.

➡ I JUST HAD MY HAIR DONE

The coiffeur equivalent of I Have a Headache, this line is also useful for avoiding outdoor activities. The unfair flaw in this excuse is that while you truly do not want to ruin what took a stylist two hours to snip and blow dry to perfection, others simply don't know (much less, appreciate) the history of your hairdo.

➡ I JUST LOOKED AWAY FOR A SECOND

There are a thousand opportunities to use this excuse—from the parent whose baby is suddenly buried in baby food to the retailer who finds his cash drawer suddenly empty.

➡ I LEFT IT AT HOME

More an explanation than an excuse, this may be useful for covering up a more flagrant problem with homework or an office project (i.e. You didn't do it in the first place), but it doesn't reflect terribly well on you.

➡ I LIKE IT THIS WAY

Many an awful meal has been consumed by a would-be chef rationalizing away burnt, undercooked, or ketchup-laden food that anyone in his right mind can see is not fit for human consumption.

➡ I MUST BE GETTING OLD

We are all going forward in time at the rate of one day per day. As such, we are getting older.

➡ I THOUGHT YOU WERE JOKING

This one's tricky. On rare occasions—when you've been asked to do a massive project with little explanation ("Make sure the apartment is clean from top to bottom before I get back")—you can get away with it. But when the matter is more serious (your best friend saying "I've love you since high school,"), then this statement—preceded by a bout of doubled-over laughter—will be a major challenge to talk your way out of.

➡ I WAS BEING IRONIC

Putting air quotes around something doesn't necessarily excuse it.

➡ I WASN'T SERIOUS

This one covers a lot of ground—from facing down the blank stares of your colleagues at work when you pitch what you thought was a brilliant idea to facing down the blank stare of your spouse at the mall after you suggest that he or she buy a particularly provocative undergarment.

➡ I WASN'T WEARING MY GLASSES

When used to explain pairing up with an undesirable partner, this will get you a little bit of clemency. When trying to cover up a car accident, it only works if your name is Mister Magoo. (See also: My Contacts Were Out)

➡ IF I TOLD YOU, I'D HAVE TO KILL YOU

Cute, but nobody takes this Mafioso/spy movie cliché seriously. Unless you know something we don't know.

➡ I'LL BORROW YOURS

Trying to get out of buying something? Just invite yourself to use your friend's. This excuse works the first time but could create problems on subsequent uses.

➡ I'M OUT OF PRACTICE

You'll get a lot more mileage out of this one if you haven't built yourself up to be great in whatever activity (golf, playing foosball, having sex) you've now been humbled by.

➡ IT JUST DISAPPEARED

You don't have to be David Blain's brother—or a believer in the supernatural—to use this excuse when working on a project that involves a computer. Everyone, it seems, has a horror story about some important file that "just" vanished, never to be found again.

The biggest downside of using this one is knowing what to say when someone invariably asks, "Didn't you save it while you were working on it?"

➡ IT SOUNDED GOOD

Yeah, it might have, but now you're committed to a movie that sucks, a meal that's inedible or a concert that's making your ears bleed.

➡ IT WAS ALREADY LIKE THAT

One of the first cover-ups a kid learns is to try to pass off a broken item as previously broken.

➡ IT WAS HERE A MINUTE AGO

Maybe. Or maybe you just lost it and are obviously trying to cover for your own lack of organizational skills.

➡ IT'S AGAINST MY RELIGION

Yeah, but so are a lot of other things that you seem willing to turn a blind spiritual eye to.

➡ IT'S ON THE NEW YORK TIMES BESTSELLER LIST

Having an awkward moment when your book club finds you deep into the latest Danielle Steele or Nicholas Sparks tome? Putting yourself in the company of a gang of other readers—and implying that the NY *Times* list somehow is the same as getting a good review in the same paper—is a quick but not terribly effective dodge. Don't be surprised if you're dropped to the bottom of the pick-the-next-book list.

➡ I'VE BEEN SWAMPED

We're all busy. Two conclusions can be drawn from that fact. One is that there's a vast world of people who understand what it is like to be busy. The other is that your excuse is likely to be met by "Yeah, so?"

➡ NO THANKS, I JUST ATE

Being offered food that looks particularly nasty? At a barbecue where the chef serves the burgers right off of the Styrofoam container that the raw meat came in? Begging off because of an already full stomach is the way to go. This should be your guiding principle when visiting friends who have certain cleanliness issues. (See also: I'm Fasting.)

➡ THE NURSE TOLD ME THIS MIGHT HAPPEN

Not a bad excuse for falling asleep at work—but it works better if your arm is sporting a bandage covering a cotton ball.

➡ THAT'S OKAY—I'LL DO IT MYSELF

Who among us has not passed on the maintenance suggestions of the oil change guy with confident-sounding self-reliance excuse? And who among us hasn't found ourselves back at the oil change place six months later with those same frayed wiper blades?

➡ THERE MUST HAVE BEEN SOME MISCOMMUNICATION

This is a great way to drag others into your personal mistake without directly blaming them directly for your blunder.

➧ YOU'RE JUST PREJUDICED/YOU JUST DON'T LIKE [FILL IN THE BLANK] PEOPLE

There's a lot of very real racism in the world. There are also those occasions—much rarer, of course—where a convenient and uncomfortable-to-argue-with excuse is that the person questioning your behavior is doing it because of racism rather than because of legitimate indignation, logic, or justified pissed-offness.

➧ THE WEATHER

Look! Up in the sky! It's a convenient excuse for tons of occasions! Too hot. Too cold. Rainy. Snowy. Typhoony. You name the weather and there's probably something it will help get you out of. Of course, you have to take into account that all of us are under that same sky.

➧ YOU'RE ACTING JUST LIKE THE KIDS WHO USED TO MAKE FUN OF ME ON THE PLAYGROUND

When your "tormentors" catch on to the fact that your negative reaction to a situation is out of proportion to the offense, you can try this one, which will either a.) lead others to sympathize with these deep-seeded negative memories, or, b.) remind them how fun it was to be a bully in elementary school and pick on wimps like you.

SCHOOL/ EDUCATION

·······EXCUSES·······

School is not only a place to learn academics. It's also a place to learn how to weasel your way out of whatever you've gotten yourself into. It can be argued that those who will find success in life aren't necessarily those who make it to the top 10 percent of their class—it's more likely that it's those who have figured out a way around whatever obstacles they've created for themselves.

➡ THE DOG ATE MY HOMEWORK

It's an excuse that—without that baggage—is relatively believable. There are dogs that do, in fact, take pleasure in consuming—or, at least, tearing apart—paper. Canines have been known to gnaw on paper towels, masticate money and destroy documents. But this one has become such a cliché that it's unlikely to ever, ever work again. Even if your dog actually does make a meal out of your American History term paper. It doesn't help that it's also becoming outdated, since hitting "print" isn't nearly as difficult as retyping a paper used to be.

One small bit of good news: If you somehow manage to get away with this one the first time, you might be able to get away with it a second. If you have a dog that likes to eat paper, chances are you aren't going to change his ways.

➡ I DIDN'T HEAR THE BELL

And your teacher doesn't care.

➡ I'LL USE CLIFFSNOTES

Bookmark on page 10 and a test on the material tomorrow? CliffsNotes have been saving the butts of students since 1958. The degree to which the excuse is acceptable is, of course, dependent upon the impression you want those you tell to have of you. In other words, context is the only thing that sometimes separates too cool for school from bonehead.

➡ I'M SELF-EDUCATED

Sure, it's better than saying "I'm stupid." But when you use this one after a particularly boneheaded comment or action, it's unlikely that anyone will think anything besides, "Then you really picked the wrong school."

➡ IT'S EDUCATIONAL

A good way to rationalize almost any activity is to pretend to find some educational value in it. Thus, "Getting high in the woods" becomes "observing the effects of chemicals on the perception of flora and fauna." Similarly, playing poker with your pals becomes "an opportunity to observe how members of a sample group, each with his or her own probability theory, reacts to a common set of circumstances."

➡ PEER PRESSURE

This excuse is rarely used on oneself. Instead, it's a standard excuse used to explain how the bad behavior of someone you like can be excused because that person has fallen under the influence of someone or a group of someones you don't like.

Thus, the reason has less to do with character flaws, overt selfishness, or criminal tendencies and much more to do with the fact that he or she has fallen in with the wrong crowd.

Of course, no one blamed peer pressure when the conformity in question involved joining a church group, defending your country, or participating in a charity event. Pressure, it seems, is in the eye of the beholder.

➡ THE SCHOOL BUS NEVER SHOWED UP

For latchkey kids whose parents have to leave for work early, this is a great excuse to stay home for the day. Just don't overuse it ... or try it if you live across the street from your school.

➡ THE TEACHER DOESN'T LIKE ME

And there are probably a couple of very good reasons for that

➡ THE TESTS ARE CULTURALLY BIASED

People much higher on the academic pecking order make such claims. And often their cases have a kernel of truth in them. But it's not going to help you get out of the "culturally biased" geometry exam you have to take.

➡ TOO MANY DISTRACTIONS

Few of us spend much time in solitary confinement. The rest have to put up with interruptions—which is why this excuse is almost universally accepted.

Of course, it's rendered meaningless if you don't follow it with actually going someplace theoretically less distracting.

In other words, "There are too many distractions here at the frat house, I'm going to the library," is more likely to be bought than, "The baby's crying. I need to think. I'm going to the strip club."

➡ WE WERE NEVER TOLD THAT WAS GOING TO BE ON THE TEST

When a school exam shows up in front of you, there really aren't a whole lot of excuses that are going to have any impact whatsoever on your ultimate schooling.

SOME ADDITIONAL
SCHOOL/ EDUCATION
EXCUSES TO ADD TO YOUR REPERTOIRE

➤ IT'S HARD TO CONCENTRATE IN A CLASS LED BY A TEACHER WHO HAS HIT ON ME ON MORE THAN ONE OCCASION.

➤ THE LESSON IS AGAINST MY RELIGION.

➤ HAMLET WOULDN'T HAVE STOOD FOR THIS ... AT LEAST, NOT AFTER HE THOUGHT ABOUT IT FOR A WHILE.

➤ YOU KNOW, WHEN YOU THINK ABOUT IT, THERE ARE ONLY A FEW SHORTS STEPS BETWEEN HALL PASSES AND TOTALITARIANISM.

S-E-X
EXCUSES

Few aspects of life provide more opportunities for awkwardness and miscommunication than sex. And where there is awkwardness and/or miscommunication, you can always find excuses.

Here, then, are excuses for dealing with those who want something that you don't, for addressing the well-known side effects (humiliation, pregnancy, et al), and for managing the uncomfortable time when the spirit is willing but the flesh doesn't seem interested.

➡ I DID IT FOR THE GOOD OF OUR RELATIONSHIP

Admittedly, the person who is caught by his significant other in the arms of a not-as-significant other is in something of a bind. Excuses are a little difficult to come by when the evidence does not support your argument.

➡ I DON'T WANT TO RUIN OUR FRIENDSHIP

Ah, that uncomfortable moment when Friend 1 expresses a romantic interest in Friend 2 only to find out that Friend 2 doesn't want to go there. Or thinks Friend 1 is really, really unappealing.

➡ I FELT SORRY FOR HIM/HER

If, on the Monday following your office Christmas party, a certain someone from a certain accounts payable department starts mooning around your desk, making comments to suggest that she has intimate knowledge of your personal life (i.e. the names of your pets and the contents of your refrigerator), then people are going to eventually put two and two together. So you'd better have a compelling story to explain away your lapse in judgment.

Painting your tryst as a humanitarian act has a certain sweetness—and might even earn you some sympathy points when you're filling out the paperwork for the restraining order.

➡ I HAVE A HEADACHE

The classic get-out-of-whoopee line.

➡ I HAVE AN IRREGULAR CYCLE

Woman's secret weapon is her cycle—that mood altering chain of events that begins with ovulation, turns into premenstrual syndrome, and culminates in full-on cramps. It's not easy being a woman, and people will cut you a lot of slack if you occasionally become bloated, moody and in need of an exorcism. But blaming Aunt Martha's visit on an unplanned pregnancy will only prove that you didn't paying attention during the filmstrip in 5th-grade health class.

➡ I THOUGHT YOU WERE USING BIRTH CONTROL

Statistically, about half of the pregnancies in the U.S. are unintended. And while a percentage of those can be chalked up to either ignorance or a consensual seizing of the moment, that still leaves a significant number of instances of after-the-fact accusations.

Unfortunately, without using birth control of any kind, 25% of sexually active women will become preggers within a month. 85% within a year.

Not a nice gambling percentage.

And let's not even get into the STDs.

Even the person desperately uttering the "I thought you were taking care of this" line while staring in shock at the results of an EPT test knows that this is a pretty lame excuse. And one that not only doesn't help the situation, but also is likely to piss off the partner who you're going to have to make some big decisions with in the near future.

➡ I WAS BREAKING A DRY SPELL

Maybe it wasn't the most prudent relational decision you've ever made. No worries. This excuse works surprisingly well when you've done something slutty. Just the mere suggestion that you went out and got your groove back generally merits a raised-fist, "you go, girl" reaction.

➽ I WAS ON THE REBOUND

There are a lot of traps you can fall into when you're in the recovery period of the big-relationship-that-went-bad. Sometimes, when getting out of one of those traps, you need an excuse. This one is not ideal, because it implies that you entered the new relationship disingenuously.

➽ I'M SORRY—THIS NEVER HAPPENED BEFORE

Actually, this excuse applies to two situations. One—how do we put this delicately?—is when things happen too quickly. The other is when things don't quite happen at all.

In both cases, either the excuse recipient is going to be sympathetic (in which case, there should be a next time) or not (in which case you probably shouldn't have been there in the first place.)

➽ IT DIDN'T REALLY MEAN ANYTHING

Anyone who has seen the movie Almost Famous or heard Snoop Dog's "Groupie" knows that there are temptations on the road for a popular musician. Anyone who has been to a hardware wholesalers convention knows that the rich and famous aren't the only ones faced with temptations when out of town (although, in the latter, there's a better chance of that temptation going by the name of "Marge"). No matter where your out of town dalliance takes place, this excuse is far from guaranteed to salvage your primary relationship. But it at least sends the message that you're not going to be pursuing Round Two with the person whose last name you never did find out.

➡ IT'S BEEN A LONG TIME

Pity is an underused but highly effective tactic when you need a pardon for not being the world's most proficient lover. So what if you fumble a bit? Everyone loves an underdog. Plus, if you set the expectations low, you'll get an A+ for effort.

➡ SHE LOOKED 18

From the classic Animal House revelation after the angel/devil scene or the "To think that in just seven months you'll be graduating from high school" moment in Old School, movies have been very sympathetic to adult guys who had a "don't ask/don't card" policy toward their romantic partners.

Real life, though, isn't likely to be as kind. Ignorance isn't going to get you off the hook with the law—or with an irate father.

➡ WE DIDN'T GO ALL THE WAY

The stumble-upon-the-scene parent may, at some point, find solace in knowing that the primary deed was not done. But for now—with clothes scattered about the room—this line isn't going to take you very far.

SOME ADDITIONAL
S-E-X EXCUSES
TO ADD TO YOUR REPERTOIRE

➤ OH, I DIDN'T KNOW WE STARTED ALREADY.

➤ IF I SLEPT WITH YOU, I'D HAVE TO DEVOUR YOU.

➤ OKAY, BUT YOU'LL HAVE TO WEAR A CONDOM.
YOU DON'T WANT TO GET WHAT I HAVE!

➤ I WAS ONLY SUGGESTING IT BECAUSE I
THOUGHT YOU WOULD ENJOY IT.

➤ IT'S NOT ABOUT YOUR APPEARANCE; IT'S
ABOUT HOW MUCH MORE CONFIDENT YOU'LL
FEEL AFTER THE ENHANCEMENT SURGERY.

➤ PLEASE DON'T TAKE IT PERSONALLY. MY
NARCOLEPSY CAN STRIKE AT ANY TIME.

EXCUSES RELATED TO
SHOPPING
and
RETAIL

If the things we bought were strictly items that were required for our sustenance and survival, there'd be some pretty empty malls and lots of bare closets.

With most of our shopping focused on the optional rather than the mandatory, it's no wonder that we need to rationalize our behavior so often—and face the challenges of those who don't think we made the proper purchasing decisions.

➨ I ALREADY RETURNED THAT

Okay, so this one isn't exactly buying—it's renting—but we couldn't fit it in anywhere else.

When you find the DVD from January under the couch in April, there's little to do short of paying the massive fine besides call up this pathetic "heard it before" refrain of DVD retailers everywhere. This line is most regrettable when it involves an embarrassing title (better for The Godfather, for instance, to haunt you than From Justin to Kelly.) Don't count on it doing more than reducing your fine a bit.

➨ I CAN ALWAYS RETURN IT

The must-have excuse for buying more than you need, this classic shifts the responsibility for selecting goods from the pre-cash-register phase to the post-bring-it-home phase. The fact is, once it's in your closet, it's unlikely to end up back at Penney's. Even if the tags are never removed.

➨ I HAD A COUPON

Something that's not worth having isn't necessarily worth having two of for the same price. Or having at half price. Or having with a free carton of milk. Or having under whatever condition is spelled out on the coupon you are armed with.

Yet when you can't make a convincing case for purchasing an item at its retail price, you might as well use this excuse to mitigate the potential domestic fallout.

➥ I LOST THE INSTRUCTIONS

You've bought the item without problem. You've brought it home. And now you can't seem to make all the pieces fit.

The fact that you are owning up to not hanging on to the necessary document speaks well of you. The fact that you lost it in the first place doesn't. A tip before this one happens to you: Many manufacturers post their instructions online. Toy company Hasbro, for instance, offers easy access to a pdf of the rules for The Mad Magazine Game, while eBay has an instruction manual for just about any sewing machine ever made, leaving this one of those excuses that leads the listener to query, "So …?"

➥ IT INCLUDED A FREE GIFT

Subscribe to a magazine you don't want and you'll get a free DVD. Fill out this credit card application and take home this cuddly bear. Become a member of your local public television station and, at the $100 level, receive a coffee mug. Buy this set of perfumes and we'll throw in a makeup case. Sign up for a year of the Sunday newspaper and get a free 2-liter soda.

Signing incentives have been around for, well, we're not quite sure how long they've been around, but at least as long as there have been items that consumers aren't really sure they want for the asking price. Whether the excuse holds water, of course, depends on how much of an added value the "free" gift really is. Was that $5 box of cereal really worth getting when all you really wanted was the plastic toy inside to shut up your bratty kid?

➡ IT LOOKED GOOD IN THE STORE

Fashionistas will tell you that fitting room lighting is cleverly aimed and positioned to make you look like Heidi Klum, no matter what unflattering ensemble you subject yourself to. But you should have known that it was the mellow side lighting that made your skin tone look so healthy and brought out the green in your eyes, and not the plaid pedal pushers.

➡ IT WAS ON SALE

With 20 percent knocked off its original price, even the most unworthy piece of merchandise starts to take on an air of desirability. Take your chances, but it should be noted that this excuse has been the impetus for an embarrassing runway marathon of fashion "don'ts." If you make the decision to subject your size 8 thighs to a pair of size 4 jeans found on the sale rack, for instance, then no claim of financial conquest will quell the disapproving stares (or hide your camel toe).

➡ SHOPPING IS GOOD FOR THE COUNTRY

Remember back in the days of WWII—okay, maybe you don't remember back in the days of WWII, but trust us on this—there was a thing called rationing. In order to help the country, good citizens were supposed to be very careful about what they bought and spent.

Not any more. Spending is now pushed as your patriotic duty. More money spent on stuff you don't need (yes, we know this book is included in that select group) means greater consumer confidence, which means a more robust economy.

Of course, this excuse only goes so far in explaining your purchase of that catamaran.

➡ THAT WAS THE STYLE BACK THEN

This one is usually dragged out when the "what the hell were you think-ing" question is asked as photo album pages are turned to those featur-ing pics from the 1960s. Or the 1970s. Or the 1980s.

➡ THERE WAS A LINE

This strategy is often used when one returns from an errand without the requested item in hand. Whether you were sent to pick up a Honey Baked Ham, or to exchange the Medium for a Large, you will get no pity from the folks back at the homestead, even if those folks back at the homestead have done nothing all day but watch soap operas and eat bonbons. Life isn't fair.

➡ THERE WAS INTEREST-FREE FINANCING

Need an excuse to buy something you can't afford? Credit companies love throwing these sorts of offers at those who don't have the money right now but want the goods right now. This one might work with your family—who can share the pleasures of your purchase—but not with the collections people who come to take it back when the bills aren't paid.

➡ THIS QUALIFIES AS AN EMERGENCY

Want to make use of that money you've been squirreling away "in case of an emergency?" All you have to do is invoke this line, which ef-fectively broadens the definition of the word "emergency" to include whatever you want to do.

➡ YOU CAN NEVER HAVE TOO MANY SHOES

Yes, you can.

➡ YOU'LL DEFINITELY WEAR IT AGAIN

Trying to pressure your bridesmaids into spending an absurd amount of money for the chartreuse cocktail dress that'll tell the world that they are your "lucky" attendants? Pull out this oft-told bit of fiction. Just don't be surprised if your ears burn for years to come.

·····SOME ADDITIONAL·····
SHOPPING/RETAIL
EXCUSES TO ADD TO YOUR REPERTOIRE

➤ I NEEDED SOMETHING OFF-ORANGE.

➤ I'M JUST BUILDING MY SHOPPING BAG COLLECTION.

➤ IF I BUY IT, I'LL HAVE FRIENDS. THAT'S WHAT IT SHOWED IN THE COMMERCIAL.

➤ I NEEDED SOMETHING TO GO WITH MY CAN-CAN DANCER UNDERPANTS.

➤ I FELL INTO THE GAP.

➤ I SHOP AT OLD NAVY BECAUSE I SUPPORT OUR TROOPS.

SPORTS EXCUSES

Excuses in sports address the minutia and the big picture.

When it comes to professional sports, there may be a "how you play the game" factor, but when contract negotiations roll around, when endorsement contracts are on the table, when television rights are being sold, it often is "whether you win or lose."

So when the team doesn't perform to expectations, the excuses fly fast and furious.

But wins and losses are usually built on smaller things. And out of those excuses arise another set of excuses.

➤ HOUSE RULES

If used with discretion, this handy fib allows you to make up just about anything during a round of golf.

➤ I GAVE IT MY BEST SHOT

What did famed motorcycle jumper Evel Knievel say when his attempt to rocket across Colorado's Snake River Canyon failed? This nugget of obviousness, an excuse-ish statement that puts guilt into anyone who challenges it. How, after all, could you expect someone to do anything better than his or her "best shot"?

➤ I KNOW I'M BETTER THAN THIS

This is a brilliant strategy. By diverting the disappointment onto your-self, you'll render it unnecessary for anyone else to think of you as a loser. No one's a tougher critic than you, and … well, it's worth a try.

➤ I LOST IT IN THE SUN

Provided there is the legitimate presence of bright sunshine, it's tough to find fault with it. However, if you are former Brooklyn Dodger/Baltimore Oriole/San Francisco Giant pitcher William "Billy" Loes, who used this wording to explain why he failed to scoop up a grounder, then you truly have guts, friend.

➤ I USE THAT BAT FOR BATTING PRACTICE

Cork bats are not allowed in Major League Baseball.

Cork, you see, makes a bat more like a superbat.

Which is why things got a little heated when the Chicago Cubs controversial slugger Sammy Sosa hit a grounder to second during a 2003 game with the Tampa Bay Devil Rays. The problem: The bat split. Inside ... you guessed it ... cork

For his indiscretion, Sosa was kicked out of the game and suspended for eight (later reduced to seven). And, of course, questions were raised about whether or not any of his 505 home runs were corkers.

"I use that bat for batting practice," he excused later. "... just to put on a show for the fans ... I like to make people happy and I do that in batting practice."

And, to his credit, he took responsibility.

"It's something that I take the blame for. It's a mistake, I know that. I feel sorry. I just apologize to everybody that are embarrassed."

Officials, of course, weren't ready to take him at his word. They confiscated and checked all of his bats. No more cork was found.

➡ IT'S A REBUILDING YEAR

From Little League through the Major Leagues, from Pee-wee Football through the NFL, from—oh, you get the idea—sports teams have their ups and downs. When the downs are particularly down, it's time to drag out this old excusitorial warhorse that is best used at the beginning of a season to lower expectations.

➡ THE REF BLEW THE CALL

When you are at just about any game with a largely hometown crowd, you can scream blame at the refs for just about anything. After all, they do make mistakes. Zebras are only human.

But—in front of anyone save true loyalists—believably assigning blame to the ref rather than the players who lost requires a game so perfectly played by the defeated team that that one call or series of calls clearly turned the tide. A muffed penalty in a football match-up with a 17-point margin just isn't going to cut it.

Note that this one is much more effective with a hometown crowd than with anyone even remotely objective.

➡ THE TEAM JUST DIDN'T HAVE ENOUGH HEART

A kindler, gentler way of saying that the losers didn't try hard enough.

➡ THAT'S NOT HOW I'M USED TO PLAYING

Similar, but less demanding, than House Rules, this excuse might, at best, get you a redo on one botched play.

➡ THESE ARE NEW CLUBS

Golf is one of the few games where blaming the equipment is fairly common and often accepted. You don't hear a hoopster pretending that there's something wrong with the ball or a hockey player holding the puck in his open palm, pretending there's something wrong with the weight. Yet a golfer can find 18-holes worth of ways to ponder his clubs, writing off an awful score. Just be careful who's in the foursome next time out.

➡ WE'RE A SMALL MARKET TEAM

Dragged out by sports management to help blame bad seasons on geography, this excuse has some basis in the real world. Smaller cities have smaller populations from which to draw paying fans, smaller companies from which to sell suites, and lower operating budgets to attract and keep big talent. Yet it gets tiring, especially to loyal small-market fans sick of watching their favorite team drop the ball.

➡ THE WIND CAUGHT IT

Maybe it did. But unless you're playing Wiffle ball and are under 12, don't try this one unless it's the middle of a hurricane.

SOME ADDITIONAL
SPORTS EXCUSES
TO ADD TO YOUR REPERTOIRE

➤ I DIDN'T KNOW THE FIRST BASE COACH WAS GIVING ME THE STEAL SIGN–I THOUGHT HE JUST LIKED ME.

➤ THE CHEERLEADERS ARE AN UNFAIR DISTRACTION.

➤ I ONLY COME FOR THE HALFTIME SHOW.

➤ **EVER SINCE BEING CUT FROM MY PEE WEE FOOTBALL TEAM, I'VE HAD DIFFICULTY WITH TEAM SPORTS.**

➤ **SORRY, I WAS THINKING ABOUT "BRIAN'S SONG" AND GOT ALL CHOKED UP.**

➤ **I DON'T EVEN LIKE THE GIPPER.**

TECHNOLOGY EXCUSES

There's now a whole generation that cannot imagine home or workplace without computers. And technological knowledge is increasing at such a rapid rate that last year's cutting edge is this year's yawner.

Such a culture change requires a whole slew of new excuses that would have seemed like alien chatter to your grandparents—assuming your grandparents aren't forwarding e-mails to you from their retirement condos in Florida.

➤ I FRIED MY MOTHERBOARD

Frankly, we have no idea what this means either, so it always works for us.

➤ I MEANT TO DELETE IT

There's a thing in a computer called memory. Unlike your memory, what gets put in the memory of a computer stays there in the same form—barring any major crashes, of course. Getting rid of something you saved requires a conscious choice.

➤ I SAW IT ONLINE

The Internet is an amazing tool for research and learning—and the greatest achievement in the history of the dissemination of false information. Everything is online, but only a small percentage of it involves those pesky things called "facts." With a few clicks, you can research the validity of just about anything. Not taking those extra click-steps can set you up to look like a gullible fool.

➤ MY COMPUTER CRASHED

Say no more.

Understood.

Claiming a crashed computer is effective in most cases because, as we become more and more dependant on our computers, we become more and more fearful that the machines will turn on us.

Oh, we don't really think they're going to consciously make choices to take over our lives or anything. We just know that we don't have a clue how they work. "Fixing" anything besides maybe—maybe—a paper jam in the printer is akin to expecting us to be able to land a jumbo jet.

One warning, though: Be careful of your computer usage immediately after using this excuse. In a world of instant messages, the truth could be uncovered pretty quickly.

→ MY PRINTER WAS JAMMED

See Crashed, My Computer.

→ TECHNICAL DIFFICULTIES

Need a leave-me-alone-about-the-details catch-all? Try this one, which had its heyday in the early years of television (usually preceded by "We are experiencing..." and followed by the encouraging "please stand by."

····· SOME ADDITIONAL ·····
TECHNOLOGICAL
EXCUSES
TO ADD TO YOUR REPERTOIRE

➤➤ SERVES ME RIGHT FOR BUYING A COMPUTER AT GOODWILL.

➤➤ THERE'S SO MUCH PORN ON MY HARD DRIVE, I'M SURPRISED ANY PROGRAMS WORK.

➤➤ I'M A LUDDITE.

➤➤ I WOULD HAVE PRINTED IT, BUT I BELIEVE IN A PAPERLESS SOCIETY.

➤➤ IPOOD.

·······EXCUSES FOR·······
TELLING A SECRET

More than just information, a secret contains the understanding that you are someone that another person trusts. Now that you've blown that trust, you'd better come up with something good.

➡ I DID IT FOR YOUR OWN GOOD

To effectively make the transition from "Former Confidant Who No Longer Can Be Trusted" to "Friend Who Sees the Big Picture in All Things" requires some delicate maneuvering and a fairly ironclad case for the positive impact of the actions of your loose lips. Good luck with that one.

➡ I HAD TO TELL SOMEONE

This excuse makes clear that the person who told you the secret in the first place didn't understand your understanding of the rules of secrecy. Now they understand. Don't count on any more juicy gossip/stock tips in the near future.

➡ IT SLIPPED

Putting the revelation of a trusted detail on par with accidentally stepping on a patch of ice, this excuse gives little to argue with but also does little to rebuilt your trust. The result is the same as the rest of the previous excuses in this section. Don't count on being trusted again for a long time.

➡ I THOUGHT I COULD TRUST HIM/HER

Well, obviously, you couldn't. You're screwed.

➡ WAIT, THAT WAS A SECRET?

A powerful dodge—the effectiveness of this one depends on how strong you are at confusing the accuser. Your mission: To convince him or her that the circumstances of the revelation did not automatically imply that a secret was being told. Pull this one off and we'll have you collaborating on future editions of this book.

➡ WHAT'S IT GOING TO MATTER IN 100 YEARS?

Good question, Mr. Philosopher. The problem is, you could apply the same logic to anything from what movie to go to to whether or not to hold the door open for a guy in a wheelchair. No, it probably won't matter in a hundred years. But it will matter as long as your reputation is shot.

SOME ADDITIONAL EXCUSES FOR
revealing a
SECRET
TO ADD TO YOUR REPERTOIRE

➤ IT WAS A MATTER OF NATIONAL SECURITY.

➤ I'D TELL YOU WHY I DID IT, BUT IT'S A SECRET.

➤ IF I DIDN'T TELL, MY LIFE WAS AT STAKE.

➤ IT WASN'T A PARTICULARLY GOOD SECRET ANYWAY. I MEAN, WHEN ARE YOU GOING TO COME UP WITH A REAL SECRET. LIKE THE ONE JIM TOLD ME ABOUT THE TIME WHEN HE AND HIS GIRLFRIEND...

WORKPLACE EXCUSES

The office arena is the perfect testing ground for possible excuses. The real challenge is that those who check your timesheet and sign your paycheck have heard them all.

➡ DIDN'T YOU GET THE MEMO?

It's never a good idea to try an excuse that posits a paper trail that doesn't exist.

➡ I DON'T KNOW WHO KEEPS FORWARDING ME THIS JUNK

Sure you do. That's why you spend half your day taking personal quizzes, watching nonsensical foreign videos, and marveling at the guy who paints those cool, hyperrealistic pictures on the sidewalk. If you plan on using this excuse in the future, make sure nobody at the office is on your own forward list.

➡ I JUST DIDN'T HAVE TIME

We've all missed deadlines or turned in half-completed work. Any of these situations imply that time was a factor. When others are given the same task and do manage to complete it, though, you're on flimsy excuse ground if you can't make a good case for why your 24 hour days weren't as manageable as everyone else's.

➡ I'M HAVING SOME PROBLEMS AT HOME

Sometimes the only fall back after a really uncomfortable office moment—shouting obscenities at a co-worker, being caught trying to lift the candy machine in an effort to shake off the dangling bag of Cheetos—is to let it be known, truthfully or not, that you are having troubles on the homefront. This may help ease tension in the short term, but in the long term, it's not great to be known as the guy who can't check his family problems at the door.

➥ IT PAYS THE BILLS

It's difficult to begrudge anyone his or her efforts to make a living. But you have to admit, it's a little less difficult when that occupation involves a pole and a g-string—and when much of the income comes in singles.

➥ IT WAS A DECISION FROM CORPORATE

Blaming the faceless corporation comes in handy for anything from massive layoffs to a policy shift that no longer sees subsidized coffee as a right.

➥ IT'S NOT MY JOB

This isn't exactly passing the buck, it's refusing to allow the buck anywhere near you by virtue of employment description. Use of this one might get you out of the line of responsibility fire in the short term, but in the long term it paints you in "not a team player" colors.

➥ IT'S UNDER THE TABLE

Not paying taxes on income is, of course, illegal. But while undocumented foreigners run the risk of being busted, it's unlikely that your teenage babysitter is going to have to face the music. That's why being paid under the table—out of sight of the IRS—makes a gig more lucrative and encourages the use of this excuse when the question arises about the meager salary or pathetic conditions.

➥ WE HAD TO CLEAN HOUSE

This one works a little better on the survivors of a purge than on those being swept to the curb.

➥ WE'VE RETHOUGHT THE POSITION

When a boss can't quite answer your question about what you've done wrong, this excuse often pops up. While the position may have been rethought, the powers that be obviously don't see you in that position any longer.

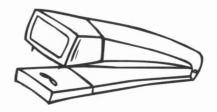

SOME ADDITIONAL
WORKPLACE
EXCUSES TO ADD TO YOUR REPERTOIRE

➤ YOU DIDN'T HEAR ABOUT THE COMPANY-WIDE ASS COPYING CONTEST?

➤ NO, I'M NOT TRYING TO TIP THE CANDY MACHINE AND SHAKE LOOSE THAT DANGLING BAG OF CHIPS. I HAVE AN ITCH IN THE SMALL OF MY BACK AND I'M TRYING TO SCRATCH IT. DIDN'T YOU EVER SEE HOW BALOO THE BEAR DID THAT WITH THE TREE IN JUNGLE BOOK?

➤ I REALLY BELIEVE THAT, BY PERSONALIZING MY CUBICLE, I'M FURTHERING THE AIMS OF THE COMPANY BY CREATING AN ENVIRONMENT THAT IS MORE LIKELY TO ATTRACT QUALITY WORKERS.

➤ BUT THEY DO IT ON THE OFFICE.

EXCUSES UTTERED BY
the
RICH
and
SHAMELESS

➡ "I made a terrible mistake. I got caught up in the excitement of the moment. I would never intentionally endanger the lives of my children." – *Michael Jackson after dangling his baby.*

➡ "I was told that I should shoplift. The director said I should try it out." – *Winona Ryder, quoted by a guard at Saks Fifth Avenue, where she was arrested for shoplifting.*

➡ "The arresting officer was just doing his job and I feel fortunate that I was apprehended before I caused injury to any other person. I acted like a person completely out of control when I was arrested, and said things that I do not believe to be true and which are despicable."
—*Mel Gibson, denying that he actually believed his previous statement that "Jews are responsible for all the wars in the world."*

➡ "Crack is cheap. I make too much money to use crack. Crack is whack."
—*Whitney Huston*

➡ "All I know is, I woke up and I am covered in cream."
— *R.E.M.'s Peter Buck*

➡ "Not to make excuses, but 600,000 of Clint's biggest fans were in the Persian Gulf fighting a war when The Rookie came out."
— *Charlie Sheen, making an excuse for the flop of The Rookie, in which he co-starred with Clint Eastwood.*

➡ "I was being a good Samaritan. It's not the first hooker I've helped out. I've seen hookers on corners ... and I'll pull over ... and they'll go, 'Oh you're Eddie Murphy, oh my God,' and I'll empty my wallet out to help."
—*Eddie Murphy, after being caught with a pre-op transsexual prostitute in his car.*

➡ "My band started playing the wrong song. I didn't know what to do so I thought I'd do a hoe-down."
– Ashley Simpson, after a guide track —which allows a singer to lip sync— began playing on Saturday Night Live. She later said that severe acid reflux caused her to lose her voice and her father talked her into relying on the tape.

➡ "I am sorry that anyone was offended by the wardrobe malfunction …"
– Justin Timberlake, attempting to explain the exposure of Janet Jackson's breast on national television and adding a phrase to the excuse lexicon.

➡ "My mistake … and it is one I deeply regret, is writing about the person I created in my mind to help me cope, and not the person who went through the experience."
–James Fry, author of the fictional non-fiction book A Million Little Pieces.

➡ "But what a lot of people don't know is that I had just finished filming The Hulk. That's the hair I had from the movie! I just finished the film and that's the way the hairdresser did my hair."
–Nick Nolte, explaining the wild 'do in his mug shot from his drunk driving arrest.

➡ "Nowadays, you can make a tape, you can make a song; it can sound like a person or look like a person … but that's not me."
–R. Kelly, disputing videotaped evidence that he had relations with a woman who was under 18.

➤ "The heart wants what it wants."
—Woody Allen, explaining why he left his wife for his wife's daughter.

➤ "I could accept some of the things that people have explained, 'stress,' 'pressure,' 'loneliness'—that that was the reason. But that would be false. In the end you have to come clean and say 'I did something dishonorable, shabby and goatish."
—Hugh Grant, baffling the media by not making up an excuse about his encounter with a Hollywood prostitute.

APPENDIX

MISCELLANEOUS EXCUSE STUFF

about excuses

➡ "An excuse is worse than a lie, for an excuse is a lie, guarded."
—*Alexander Pope*

➡ "He that is good for making excuses is seldom good for anything else."
—*Benjamin Franklin*

➡ "We have forty million reasons for failure, but not a single excuse."
—*Rudyard Kipling*

➡ "It is better to offer no excuse than a bad one."
—*George Washington*

➡ "Any excuse will serve a tyrant."
—*Aesop*

➡ "I attribute my success to this—I never gave or took any excuse."
–*Florence Nightingale*

➡ "Difficulty is the excuse history never accepts."
–*Edward R. Murrow*

➡ "Apology is only egotism wrong side out."
–*Oliver Wendell Holmes*

➡ "And oftentimes excusing of a fault doth make the fault the worse by the excuse."
–*William Shakespeare*

MONOSYLLABIC
· · · · · · · · · EXCUSES · · · · · · · · ·

Sometimes you don't have the memory or the brainpower to compose a reasonable excuse. In that case, a syllable or two might be enough—kind of a conversational place holder—until you can compose something better.

SOME MONOSYLLABIC POSSIBILITIES:
➡ Oops
➡ Oopsy-Daisy
➡ Woops
➡ Uh-oh
➡ Uh…¨

AND A FEW SEMI-SYLLABIC:
➡ My Bad
➡ Uh-oh Spaghetti-O
➡ Oh, crap
➡ What?

The MUSICAL EXCUSE
MIX TAPE
(with something for everyone)

- ➡ "Blame Canada" *from the original soundtrack of the movie South Park: Bigger, Longer, Uncut*
- ➡ "No One is to Blame" *by Howard Jones*
- ➡ "Excuses" *by Alanis Morissette*
- ➡ "No Excuses" *by Alice in Chains*
- ➡ "Blame" *by Korn*
- ➡ "My Fault" *by Eminem*
- ➡ "Don't Blame Me" *by Cole Porter*
- ➡ "It's Your Fault" *from the Broadway musical "Into the Woods"*
- ➡ "Making Excuses" *by Marty Robbins*
- ➡ "Blame It on the Weatherman" *by B *witched*
- ➡ "Blame It on My Youth" *by Frank Sinatra*
- ➡ "Excuse Me (I Think I've Got a Heartache)" *by Buck Owens.*

➥ INDEX TO MAJOR EXCUSES

"Am I My Brother's Keeper?"   83

As Long as You're Playing, You Get Free Drinks   53

Because I'm Your Mother, That's Why   131

Because It's There   76

Because That's Where They Keep The Money   77

Big Government   148

But I Saw The Movie   156

But I Sent You an Invitation   156

But I Was Winning   53

Camera Adds 10 Pounds, The   26

Didn't You Get the Memo?   202

Dog Ate My Homework, The   165

Everybody Does/Is Doing It   83

Exhaustion   110

Female Trouble   110

Gerbil Must Have Crawled Up There All By Itself, The   110

God Told Me To   101

Hair of the Dog   136

He and His Girlfriend Haven't Been Getting Along   38

He Just Fell in With the Wrong Crowd   131

He Started It   83

He That Smelt It, Dealt It   118

He Was Always Quiet and Never Any Trouble   101

He Was Asking for It   156

He/She Was Asking For It   101

He's Going through a Separation   38

He's Just Going to Spend It on Drugs or Booze   65

Her Husband's a Workaholic   38

House Rules   186
How Did That Get There?   156
I Acted in Self-defense   101
I Actually Prefer an Eclectic Look   70
I Already Returned That   178
I Am Not a Crook   148
I Am What I Am   11
I Came From a Broken Home   102
I Can Always Return It   178
I Can't Eat Shellfish   93
I Could Win a Prize   59
I Couldn't Get a Cab   88
I Couldn't Get Tickets   47
I Couldn't Hold It In/Better Out Than In   118
I Did It for the Good of Our Relationship   171
I Did It for Your Own Good   197
I Did Not Have Sex With That Woman   149
I Didn't Get a Chance   11
I Didn't Get Enough Love as a Child   11
I Didn't Hear the Bell   165
I Didn't Know It Was Loaded   102
I Didn't Need Hand-Outs   65
I Didn't Realize How Fast I Was Going   98
I Didn't Want It to Go Bad   124
I Don't Have Any Clean Clothes   156
I Don't Have Anything to Wear   33
I Don't Know What They're Teaching Her in That School   131
I Don't Know Who Keeps Forwarding Me This Junk   202
I Don't Like Any of the Candidates   149
I Don't Like You in That Way   142

I Don't Want to Ruin Our Friendship   171

I Don't Wear a Watch   88

I Fell Asleep   18

I Felt Sorry for Him/Her   171

I Floss Every Day   111

I Followed the Recipe   70

I Forgot   11

I Forgot It Was Daylight Savings Time   18

I Fried My Motherboard   193

I Gave at the Office   65

I Gave It My Best Shot   186

I Get It For the Articles   78

I Got Bad Directions   88

I Got the Date Wrong   18

I Had a Bad Day   12

I Had a Coupon   178

I Had a Doctor's Appointment   18

I Had a Lousy Lawyer   102

I Had a Run of Bad Luck   53

I Had a Two-for-One   124

I Had Bad Representation   26

I Had the Wrong Address   89

I Had to Tell Someone   197

I Have a Headache   171

I Have a System   54

I Have an Irregular Cycle   172

I Have Bad Knees   98

I Have the Munchies   124

I Have Too Much Homework   83

I Haven't Had My Coffee   156

I Heard It From a Reliable Source   157
I Just Didn't Have Time   202
I Just Don't Have Time to Exercise   124
I Just Had a Really Bad Breakup and I'm Taking Some Time Off   142
I Just Had My Hair Done   157
I Just Keep It On So It's Not So Quiet Around Here   70
I Just Looked Away for a Second   157
I Knew I Should Have Stopped for Gas   47
I Know I'm Better Than This   186
I Learned It from You   83
I Left It At Home   157
I Like It This Way   157
I Lost It in The Sun   186
I Lost the Instructions   179
I Lost Your Number   142
I Meant to Delete It   293
I Must Be Getting Old   158
I Must Have Stepped in Something   118
I Must Have Taped Over It   70
I Need to Check My Calendar   142
I No Speak English   65
I Saw It in a Movie/TV Show   102
I Saw It Online   193
I Skipped Lunch   125
I Think I Have Mono   33
I Think I Have the Flu   111
I Think I've Got Food Poisoning   112
I Thought I Could Trust Him/Her   197
I Thought It Would Be Good for My Career   26
I Thought You Were Joking   158

I Thought You Were Using Birth Control   172
I Threw My Back Out   33
I Use that Bat for Batting Practice   186
I Was Being Ironic   158
I Was Breaking a Dry Spell   172
I Was Dared   59
I Was Distracted by the Paparazzi   26
I Was Doing Research   26
I Was Drunk   12
I Was Going Through an Experimental Phase   59
I Was in College   60
I Was In Love   143
I Was in the Shower   19
I Was Nervous   125
I Was on Spring Break   60
I Was on the Rebound   173
I Was Only Going to Be in the Store for a Minute   99
I Wasn't Getting a Signal   19
I Wasn't Serious   158
I Wasn't Wearing My Glasses   158
If I Told You, I'd Have to Kill You   159
I'll Borrow Yours   159
I'll Try Anything Once   12
I'll Use Cliff's Notes   165
I'm a Christian Scientist   112
I'm a Minor   103
I'm Allergic to Cats   112
I'm Big Boned   125
I'm Celebrating   136
I'm Defrosting the Fridge Tomorrow   71

I'm Doing This For Your Own Good   131
I'm Fasting   20
I'm Feeling a Little Queasy   93
I'm Glucose Intolerant   93
I'm Going to Take Care of All of That This Weekend   71
I'm Having a Bad Hair Day   20
I'm Having Some Problems at Home   202
I'm Innocent by Reason of Insanity   103
I'm Just a Kid. What Do You Expect?   84
I'm Just Bloated   125
I'm Just Doing the Work that Nobody Else Will   104
I'm Lactose Intolerant   93, 118
I'm Not a Sell-Out   27
I'm Not Feeling Well   13
I'm Not Sure What It Is, But I Won't Get the Tests Back Until Tuesday 113
I'm Out of Practice   159
I'm Researching a Paper for My Pop Culture Class   42
I'm Seeing Someone   143
I'm Self-Educated   165
I'm Sorry—This Never Happened Before   173
I'm Still Hung Over from Last Night   33
I'm Trying a New Deodorant   118
I'm Working on It   13
I've Been Swamped   160
I've Got a Lot of Irons in the Fire   28
In Many Cultures, That's a Compliment   119
It Didn't Really Mean Anything   173
It Has Sentimental Value   71
It Included a Free Gift   179
It Just Disappeared   159

It Looked Good in the Store   180
It Must be Lost in the Mail   79
It Must Have Been Demagnetized   47
It Must Have Been the Dog   119
It Pays the Bills   203
It Should Be Legal   104
It Slipped   197
It Sounded Good   159
It Was a Decision from Corporate   203
It Was Already Like That   160
It Was Here a Minute Ago   160
It Was on Sale   180
It Was Supposed to Be a Joke   60
It's a Rebuilding Year   187
It's a Victimless Crime   99
It's Against My Religion   160
It's Been a Long Time   174
It's Best for the Kids   143
It's Educational   166
It's Just a Guilty Pleasure   42
It's Legal   104
It's Legal in Canada   104
It's My Allergies   113
It's My Asthma   113
It's My Metabolism   126
It's Necessary for National Security   149
It's No More a Drug Than Caffeine   99
It's No Use. He Won't Listen to Me   132
It's Not Hurting Anybody But Myself   136
It's Not My Fault   13

It's Not My Job   203

It's Not You, It's Me   144

It's On the New York Times Bestseller List   160

It's the First Nice Day   20

It's the Nurse's/Intern's/Resident's Fault   113

It's Tradition   137

It's True to the Character/It's in Good Taste/It's Artistically Valid   27

It's Uncomfortable   100

It's Under the Table   203

It's Usually Cleaner than This   72

It's What People Want   28

I've Been Swamped   160

I've Been Taking Cold Medicine/I'm On Antibiotics   61

I've Got a Lot of Irons in the Fire   28

I've Got Two Left Feet   48

Jesus Drank Wine   137

Life's Too Short   14

Light Was Yellow, The   100

Mathematical Error   100

Meter Was Broken, The   100

Money Doesn't Grow on Trees   66

My Alarm Must Have Been Broken   21

My Car Doors Were Frozen Shut   21

My Computer Crashed   193

My Dinner Isn't Sitting Well   94

My Handlers Took Everything I Had   28

My Landlord Sucks   72

My Opponent Started the Negative Campaigning   149

My Parents Bought It for Me   72

My Phone Must Have Been off the Hook   21

My Printer was Jammed   194
My Vote Doesn't Matter   149
No Thanks, I Just Ate   161
Nurse Told Me This Might Happen, The   161
Partisan Gridlock   150
Peer Pressure   166
Police Brutality   105
Ref Blew the Call, The   187
School Bus Never Showed Up, The   166
She Doesn't Deserve Him   38
She Looked 18   174
Shopping is Good for the Country   180
Signal is Breaking Up, The   34
Sure, Sign Me Up For (Click)   66
Teacher Doesn't Like Me, The   167
Team Just Didn't Have Enough Heart, The   188
Technical Difficulties   194
Tests are Culturally Biased, The   167
That Was the Style Back Then   181
That's How I Was Brought Up   132
That's Not How I'm Used to Playing   188
That's Okay—I'll Do It Myself   161
There Must Have Been Some Miscommunication   161
There Was a Death in the Family   22
There Was a Line   181
There Was Interest-Free Financing   181
There Was Nothing Else On   42
There Was Unbelievable Traffic   89
These Are My Skinny Jeans   126
These Are New Clubs   188

They Must Have Changed Chefs   48

They Were Stuck Together   126

They're Low-Fat   126

This Guitar is So Out of Tune   48

This Qualifies As an Emergency   181

Those Aren't My Real Parents   84

Too Many Distractions   167

Traffic Was at a Crawl   22

Wait, That Was a Secret?   197

Weapons of Mass Destruction   150

Weather, The   162

Weather Kept People Away from the Polls, The   150

We Didn't Go All the Way   174

We Had to Clean House   204

We Have to Get the Kids to Bed   94

We Needed the Eggs   77

We Were Never Told That Was going to be on the Test   167

We're a Small Market Team   188

We've Rethought the Position   204

What's It Going to Matter in 100 Years?   198

Wind Caught It, The   189

You Can Never Have Too Many Shoes   182

You Have Something on Your Blouse, Right There...Oh, It's Gone   48

You'll Definitely Wear It Again   182

You're Acting Just Like the Kids Who Used to
    Make Fun of Me on the Playground   162

You're Just Not My Type   144

You're Just Prejudiced/You Just Don't Like [Fill in the Blank] People   162

You're Only Young Once   137

You're Supposed to Honor Your Mother and Father   132

➥ ABOUT THE AUTHORS

LOU HARRY is not ashamed to admit that he is the co-author of *The High-Impact Infidelity Diet:* a novel. He is also at least partial responsible for *The Encyclopedia of Guilty Pleasures, Dirty Words of Wisdom, The X-Mas Men,* and *Creative Block.* He also takes the blame for his four children and for his work as editor-in-chief of *Indy Men's Magazine.*

JULIA SPALDING is a writer and editor who has penned a variety of articles for a variety of magazines. She co-authored *The Encyclopedia of Guilty Pleasures,* which is quite an accomplishment considering that she's been swamped, has had too many distractions (including a jammed printer), and often feels like she's coming down with the flu.

If you invite either of them to your book club meeting, don't be surprised if they show up a little late. You can reach them at <u>workforlou@aol.com</u>.